"As practical as it is profound, *Sex, Romance, and the Glory of God* may well be the best book on marriage I've ever read. Though it is little in size, it packs a huge spiritual punch. I was motivated to love my wife more and broadened in my understanding of how loving my wife brings glory to God. This book deserves to take its place among those special few known as classics, in which God reveals His truth in an uncommonly powerful way (and isn't it time that a book on sex entered that esteemed list?). If I sound enthusiastic, I am—this book is truly a treasure."

> —GARY THOMAS, author of *Sacred Marriage* and
> *Sacred Parenting*

"C. J. Mahaney has become one of the voices I have come to depend on for wise, practical counsel on applying the Scriptures to the issues that confront us. Once again in this book, he shows how the message of the gospel is central to everything we do. When so many of us have lost our biblical moorings, C. J. shows that to 'do all to the glory of God' includes everything we do—eating, drinking, even romance and sex!

"Men, if you are looking for a book that will give you a few easy tips for spicing up your sex life, look somewhere else. This book invites you instead to completely revolutionize your romantic relationship with your wife. It calls all of us to a more profound and deeply satisfying kind of countercultural sex than most of us have ever experienced."

> —BOB LEPINE
> Co-host *FamilyLife Today*
> Author of *The Christian Husband*

AIR MAIL
PAR AVION

SEX, ROMANCE, AND THE GLORY OF GOD

What Every Christian Husband Needs to Know

C.J. MAHANEY

With a Word to Wives from
CAROLYN MAHANEY

:: CROSSWAY®
WHEATON, ILLINOIS

Sex, Romance, and the Glory of God: What Every Christian Husband Needs to Know

Copyright © 2004 by Sovereign Grace Ministries

Published by Crossway
      1300 Crescent Street
      Wheaton, Illinois 60187

Cover design: Josh Dennis

First printing, 2004

Printed in the United States of America

Unless otherwise indicated, Scripture quotations are taken from the ESV®
(*The Holy Bible: English Standard Version*®), copyright © 2001 by Crossway.
Used by permission.

Scripture quotations indicated as from the NIV are taken from *The Holy Bible: New International Version*®. Copyright © 1973, 1978, 1984 by International Bible Society. Used by permission of Zondervan Publishing House. All rights reserved. The "NIV" and "New International Version" trademarks are registered in the United States Patent and Trademark Office by International Bible Society. Use of either trademark requires the permission of International Bible Society.

Scripture quotations indicated as from the NASB are taken from the *New American Standard Bible*, copyright © 1960, 1962, 1963, 1968, 1971, 1972, 1973, 1975, 1977 by The Lockman Foundation and are used by permission.

ISBN-13: 978-1-58134-624-4
ISBN-10: 1-58134-624-7
ePub ISBN: 978-1-4335-1713-6
PDF ISBN: 978-1-4335-1219-3
Mobipocket ISBN: 978-1-4335-0863-9

Library of Congress Cataloging-in-Publication Data

Mahaney, C. J.
   Sex, romance, and the glory of God : what every Christian husband needs to know / C. J. Mahaney, with Kevin Meath ; with a word to wives from Carolyn Mahaney.
      p.   cm.
   Includes bibliographical references.
   ISBN 13: 978-1-58134-624-4
   ISBN 10: 1-58134-624-7 (tpb : alk. paper)
   1. Spouses—Religious life. 2. Sex—Religious aspects—Christianity. 3. Marriage—Religious aspects—Christianity. 4. Bible. O.T. Song of Solomon—Criticism, interpretation, etc. I. Meath, Kevin. II. Mahaney, Carolyn, 1955– . III. Title.
BV4596.M3M345   2004
248.5'425—dc22   2004007743

Crossway is a publishing ministry of Good News Publishers.

VP		27	26	25	24	23	22	21	20	19	18	17
24	23	22	21	20	19	18	17	16	15	14	13	12

To Carolyn,
with all my love

When I see you in a crowd,
you're the only one who appears in color—
the rest of the world is black-and-white to me

CONTENTS

CHAPTER ONE:
GREAT SEX TO THE GLORY OF GOD   9
Deeply Satisfying Intimacy Is the Inheritance of
Every Christian Couple

CHAPTER TWO:
THE DIVINE PURPOSE FOR YOUR MARRIAGE   19
A Profound Mystery, Revealed for All to See

CHAPTER THREE:
LEARNING, LEADING, AND LOVING   27
Before You Touch Her Body, Touch Her Heart and Mind

CHAPTER FOUR:
HOW TO MAKE IT ALL HAPPEN   37
Seven Surefire Ways to Kindle Romance

CHAPTER FIVE:
THE LANGUAGE OF ROMANCE   55
Winning Your Wife with Carefully Composed Words

CHAPTER SIX:
THE GIFT OF MARITAL INTIMACY   73
A Holy Immersion in Erotic Joy

CHAPTER SEVEN:
STRONG AS DEATH   91
The Enduring Power of Covenant Love

A WORD TO WIVES FROM CAROLYN MAHANEY   105

RESOURCE MATERIALS   129

NOTES   137

CHAPTER ONE

GREAT SEX TO THE
GLORY OF GOD

*Deeply Satisfying Intimacy
Is the Inheritance of
Every Christian Couple*

A smile crossed the king's face as he dipped his quill into the inkwell one last time. With firm, smooth strokes the final lines flowed freely onto the parchment.

Pushing back from his writing desk, he sighed with satisfaction. The project had gone very well. This was some fine work. Rising from the chair and lifting his hands to heaven, Solomon, the son of David, offered thanks to the Lord. Here, complete at last, was his greatest song, one of the most important pieces of writing he had ever done. With satisfaction he lowered his eyes to the finished work spread out before him. Today we call it the Song of Solomon (or the Song of Songs).

It's about sex.

In his lifetime Solomon would produce three thousand proverbs and more than a thousand songs and hymns. The son of a legendary king, and a great king himself, he would be esteemed in Scripture as the wisest man who had yet lived. And his Song of Songs is nothing less than an explicit and unblushing celebration of sex within marriage.

To Solomon, this may have been simply a deeply personal reflection on love. But really it was much more than that. Because one day, as we know, it would be counted among the perfect and infallible words of Scripture, inerrantly inspired by the Holy Spirit and intended by God as a primary source of guidance for mankind until the return of the Son.

That's right, gentlemen. Solomon's Song of Songs is an entire book of the Bible devoted to the promotion of sexual intimacy within the covenant of marriage. It's an eight-chapter feast of unbridled, uninhibited, joyous immersion in verbal and physical expressions of passion between a man and a woman.

Not a couple of verses. Not a chapter or two. God didn't consider that enough. He decided to give us a whole book!

But can the Song of Songs really be about sex? Isn't the Bible about, well, spiritual stuff?

It sure is. And sexual intimacy within marriage has profound spiritual significance. In fact, in the next chapter we're going to take a quick look at what the Bible says about marriage. We'll see that, above all else, marriage is spiritual.

For now, though, let's put ourselves back in King Solomon's study. As husbands, we need to be clear about what this book is telling us. And when you want to understand what the Bible really means, you have to start with what the original writer actually meant. So I want us to take a moment to try to see through Solomon's eyes.

REAL PEOPLE, REAL BODIES

When Solomon was writing his Song, what do you think he had in mind?

The question is important because some Christians see Solomon's Song as a book of symbolism. Men more godly than I—and a lot smarter—have believed that this book of the Bible, if it's about marriage at all, is only about marriage in a secondary way. They understand the book primarily as an allegory or as typology. That is, they see all its talk of love and longing as symbolic of the relationship between Christ and the Church or between Christ and the soul of the individual believer.

Maybe that's how you see Solomon's Song. If so, please understand—while I don't share that view, I'm not attacking or ridiculing you or anyone else.

But I am going to take a few sentences to try to persuade you otherwise!

There are five reasons why I think the Song of Songs is exactly what it appears to be: a celebration of marital intimacy.

1) Solomon's topic was obviously sex. Just consider all the sensual and erotic language in this book! It certainly *looks* like it's about physical and emotional passions. It sure seems like this is the story of a real man and a real woman with real human bodies. When Solomon was at his desk writing the Song, do you think he had in mind some symbolic, spiritualized relationship between God and his chosen ones? I don't.

2) The Bible never suggests that this book isn't primarily about sex. No New Testament writer (or Old Testament writer, for that matter) suggests that this book, which seems so obviously to be about sex, ought to be understood primarily

as an illustration of spiritual realities. This compels me to read Solomon's Song according to the plain meaning of the words.

3) God's relationship with man is not sexual. The Song is full of erotic phrases; yet our relationship with God is never portrayed in the Bible as erotic.

The Church certainly *is* the Bride of Christ. But although the marriage between Christ and his Bride will be many unimaginably wonderful things, it will not involve sexuality.

Will it be extraordinarily and supernaturally intimate? Yes. Infinitely rewarding and fulfilling? Absolutely. But not physically erotic.

When describing our relationship with God, or when communicating our passion for him in prayer or worship, it's right to use a vocabulary of love. But this language should never include anything erotic. "God is spirit, and those who worship him must worship him in spirit and truth" (John 4:24).

4) Spiritualizing the book doesn't work. When many of the passages from Solomon's Song are viewed as symbolic statements, the results can get very strange.

In chapter 1, verse 2, we read, "Let him kiss me with the kisses of his mouth! For your love is better than wine." Now that sounds an awful lot like a particular woman saying she wants to be kissed by a particular man. But some commentators say that this verse is actually about a spiritual yearning for the Word of God.

Verse 13 of that chapter says, "My beloved is to me a sachet of myrrh that lies between my breasts." Some commentators find in this passage a reference to Christ appearing between the Old and New Testaments.

Guys, I'm no scholar, but I don't think so!

Jumping ahead to chapter 7, verse 7, we find, "Your stature is like a palm tree, and your breasts are like its clusters." Again, one commentator—a godly and sincere person, I have no doubt—suggests that in this passage "breasts" refers to the nurturing effect that sound biblical teaching has upon the Church.

You know, that idea never occurred to me. When the man says to the woman that her breasts are like fruit on a palm tree, it seems to me he's talking about . . . her breasts!

Spiritualizing the Song of Solomon just doesn't make sense. What's worse, it denies to us the powerful impact that God intends for it to have on our marriages.

5) We need instruction on sexuality. If marriage is immensely important to God (and it is), and if sex is a marvelous gift from God to married couples (which it is), it's entirely appropriate for God to tell us in Scripture how to understand and enjoy it.

In fact, how could God leave us, his most beloved creatures, on our own when it comes to something as powerful and universal as sexuality? Would he give us such a gift without also giving us guidance? Where is a Christian couple supposed to look for a model of God-glorifying sexuality? If not to Scripture, where? To Hollywood? Pop culture? Pornography?

We must not, cannot take our sexual cues from the sinful impulses of ourselves or others. And we don't have to. God has not left us in the dark. Scripture illuminates the path of marital intimacy. The Song of Solomon shines brightly, showing us the way to the best sex we can possibly experience.

Guidance . . . on sex? From the God who made us? From he who established marriage as an institution and came up with the whole fantastic idea of sex? Now that is guidance we ought to receive eagerly.

Prepare to Celebrate

So I trust my point is clear. I don't believe the Song of Solomon is primarily allegory or typology. I don't believe it is drama. I do not believe it is an elaborate diary entry. I agree with this perspective offered by the biblical commentator Lloyd Carr: "The lover and the beloved are just ordinary people."[1]

Tom Gledhill, in his commentary, puts it this way: "The two lovers are Everyman and Everywoman."[2] That's encouraging. The Song's about your marriage and mine. These eight chapters of Scripture can speak to us and, in doing so, make a dramatic difference in our lives, for the glory of God.

Passion Undefiled

There are a few experiences in this life that seem to me to have been undiminished by that first sin in the Garden of Eden. Lobster with melted butter comes to mind. So does chocolate. But at the top of the list is having sex with my wife. When I am making love to Carolyn, it's difficult for me to imagine that Adam and Eve, prior to the Fall, ever had a better time than we can have right here in the twenty-first century.

Maybe they did have a better time; I'm not sure. But I *am* sure that sex itself, in the context of marriage, is not sinful. Because sex outside of marriage is so clearly sinful, it's easy to imagine that the purity of sex within marriage must also have been tarnished—at least a little—by the Fall. But it hasn't. Not in the slightest. Man in his sinfulness may distort it, but in the context of marriage, sex itself remains an unblemished, untainted gift from God.

When we are told that "the marriage bed," an obvious reference to sexuality, is to be "undefiled" (Hebrews 13:4), we're reminded that sex in marriage is intended by God to be a pure and good thing. Even though it's intensely physical, it is not the least bit unspiritual. When a married couple is in the midst of enjoying sexual relations, they may not be experiencing holiness in the same way they experience it when praying or worshiping God, but make no mistake—that is a very holy moment.

It is God's desire that every Christian couple, including you and your wife, regularly enjoy the best, most intimate, most satisfying sexual relations of which humans are capable. We're talking really, really good sex. Marital intimacy is God's gift to those who enter his holy covenant of marriage. And what a gift it is! With the obvious exception of the gospel itself, this strikes me as some of the best news man (and woman) could ever receive!

The purpose of the book you hold in your hands is to lead us back into God's ideal of joyful, unashamed, indulgent, loving sexuality in the context of marriage. If your marriage is lacking in the passion department, God—ever-loving, ever-merciful—is eager to unfold for you and your wife new levels of intimate joy and satisfaction. If that area of your marriage is already cooking along quite nicely, don't think for a minute that you've "arrived." No matter how romantic you and your wife are, there is more. Much more.

MEN, WE MUST LEAD

As husbands, it all starts with us.

Obviously, this book is directed primarily to men. As a man, it's not ideal for me to teach women on this subject. Even when Carolyn and I present this material in a marriage seminar, 90 percent of my teaching is directed to the husbands. That's because it is your role, not mine, to lead your wife into a fuller understanding of what Scripture teaches about your sexual relationship.

However, your wife is obviously a key player in all this! Clearly, she must be actively involved if this book is to make much of a difference in your marriage. So at the end of this book Carolyn has some vitally important things to say to your wife. When you've finished reading these chapters, ask your wife to read Carolyn's "A Word to Wives" at the end of this book. You may also wish to review other portions of this book with your wife.

And, guys, the hard truth is that growth is only possible as we humble ourselves. One absolutely necessary path to humility is to ask your wife to evaluate you. So let me recommend that you invite her to help you in this area. Say to her something like, "If you knew that I would not react with sinful anger, how would you evaluate me as a husband and a lover? Please be completely honest."

In my pride, I'm usually all too confident that in most areas—including my marriage—I'm probably doing a fine job. Typically, reality only dawns when I bring my wife into the evaluation process. Throughout our almost thirty years of marriage, very little growth in godliness has occurred in my life without Carolyn's encouragement, correction, and involvement.

I'd be remiss at this point if I didn't add that the encouragement, correction, and involvement of many fellow pastors and friends over the years has also been invaluable for our marriage. You, too, will need the care and biblical counsel of your pastor and godly friends in order to benefit fully from what you read in this book. We all do. Growth in marriage, like growth in godliness, does not take place in isolation from the local church.[3] Your involvement and participation in a genuine local church will be a unique and necessary means of grace in your marriage.

But most importantly, as you read through this book, let it initiate many helpful discussions with your wife on many vital topics. And may your discussions be regularly followed by the pleasures of application.

Before we look in some detail at the Song of Solomon, however, we must examine the ultimate purpose of marriage, and we must learn to love and lead our wives in the cultivation of romance. Only then will we truly be prepared to benefit fully from Solomon's wisdom in this area. As the two of you allow that unique book of Scripture to affect how you pursue marital intimacy, Solomon's Song can become your song too, bringing much joy to your marriage and great glory to God.

The Scriptures aren't sour on sex, you know. They view marital relations as a source of legitimate, godly joy and satisfaction—a holy gift from God. Since our wedding day in May 1975, Carolyn and I have been happily verifying that with repeated personal experience. No, sex in marriage is not merely to be tolerated, but actively celebrated! And Solomon's Song does exactly that.

That's what we'll be doing in this book, guys. We're going to learn what Scripture teaches us on this subject—what God thought was most important for us to know about sex within marriage. As we learn, we're going to lead our wives into increasingly rich, erotic, holy, satisfying, God-glorifying encounters!

CHAPTER TWO

THE DIVINE PURPOSE
FOR YOUR MARRIAGE

A Profound Mystery, Revealed for All to See

*W*hy am I here? *What is the purpose of my existence?* We've all asked ourselves those questions in one way or another.

When we become Christians, the answer begins to take shape. The truly converted man knows he is here because of God and for God. But we can still wonder how to really nail it down—what is the purpose of the Christian's existence? Probably the best answer I've heard is hundreds of years old: "To glorify God and to enjoy him forever."[4]

That's an excellent, brief answer to a most important question. But if you're a Christian husband, there ought to be a related question occupying your thoughts.

What is the purpose of my marriage?

After all, God has given you a wife. You are now one flesh with her. The two of you are joined together at the deepest possible level.

So, do you know the answer to that question? Do you realize your marriage has a God-given purpose?

Maybe you have been drawn to this book because you feel your marriage could use more sexual spark. Thanks to the Bible's teaching on marriage, especially that which is found in Solomon's Song, I believe that spark is available for you to discover and experience.

But if this book discussed sex without first answering the critical question, *What is the purpose of my marriage?* it would only encourage our sinful tendency to relate to our wives selfishly rather than serving them for the glory of God. You see, sex is never supposed to be treated as simply a means of personal fulfillment. Sex is derived from marriage. It's intended to serve marriage, and never to be separated from marriage. It's about man and wife in loving, complementary, erotic relationship. It is this kind of sex—taking place within marriage and informed by a biblical understanding of sex and marriage—that brings maximum joy to the couple and genuine glory to God.

Of course, secular culture seeks sexual fulfillment in isolation from God's wisdom, promising men and women all the enduring enjoyment of sexuality without the context that God designed for it. But that worldly promise always falls short because the One who created sex won't let it be fulfilled!

The best sex and the deepest human intimacy are only possible when, first, sex takes place within the context of marriage, and, second, that couple is living in the light of God's purpose for marriage. That is simply how God designed it. And this is why we need to take part of this chapter to clarify that second point—God's purpose for marriage.

ADAM, MOSES, AND PAUL

We've all sat in weddings and heard these words from Genesis 2:24: "Therefore a man shall leave his father and his mother and hold fast to his wife, and they shall become one flesh."

That's a very popular passage to read at weddings. But it's not the whole story.

Genesis 2:24 shows that God instituted marriage when Eve was presented to Adam. It tells us that in marriage a man and a woman begin a new life together—a life even closer than the relationship between parents and children. And it tells us that in marriage, physical intimacy is approved by God. But the verse doesn't pre-sent the whole picture about the purpose of marriage.

When Moses first wrote those words, his understanding was limited. God's saving purposes for man were still unfolding. Jesus had not yet come to give up his life on the cross for the sins of the world. The New Testament Church had not yet been established. But after all these things had taken place, God revealed to the apostle Paul the ultimate purpose for marriage that had been planned prior to the beginning of time.

In Ephesians 5:22-33 Paul explains that glorious purpose. He begins by instructing wives how to submit to their husbands ("as to the Lord") and husbands how to love their wives ("as Christ loved the church"). Finally, he caps it all off by quoting Genesis 2:24 and giving us its ultimate meaning.

> *"Therefore a man shall leave his father and mother and hold fast to his wife, and the two shall become one flesh." This mystery is profound, and I am saying that it refers to Christ and the church.*
>
> EPHESIANS 5:31-32

As we consider these verses, we might not be immediately inspired. We might be thinking things like, *What exactly is Paul talking about? I may not be the sharpest knife in the drawer, but I don't really see what's so profound here. Plus, if it's a mystery, how can I understand it?*

It's important to realize what Paul means by "mystery." The word shows up several times in his New Testament letters, and not once does it mean something incomprehensible or impossible to understand. Instead, Paul uses the word to refer to a particular kind of truth—a truth that, for a time, God kept hidden from man but that he has now revealed. For Paul, "mystery" is revealed truth, made plain and understandable.

So in Ephesians 5—the most significant and remarkable passage of Scripture about marriage—Paul quotes Genesis 2:24, and then he tells us there was a hidden truth in that verse. He tells us it's a "profound" truth. And he tells us what that truth is. It's what he has been explaining since verse 22.

Marriage between a man and a woman is meant to reflect the relationship between Christ and the Church.

That relationship between Christ and the Church is certainly profound and amazing. Christ came to earth as a man, lived a perfect life, and died on the cross for our sins, taking the punishment we so richly deserved. He is now in heaven interceding for us and will one day return to take us as his own. In the meantime the Church depends on him, serves him, and seeks to glorify him in all of life.

In Ephesians 5 Paul is saying, in effect, "Guess what, your marriage is kind of like that!"

So, although this truth about your marriage is something you can understand, it still ought to be profoundly mysterious and amazing, for it makes your marriage as holy a human relationship as one can imagine.

At one time I did not see my marriage as profound, mysterious, or amazing. In my ignorance I saw Carolyn and myself simply as two married people who loved God and one another.

I had not yet grasped the bigger picture that God had revealed to Paul: By God's grace and power, marriage can reflect, in some real yet imperfect way, the relationship between Christ and the Church. There are many profound implications to this truth. To really understand it is to find your entire marriage beginning to change in rich and wonderful ways—including in the bedroom.

LIVING THE MYSTERY

Paul reveals to us in Ephesians 5 the divine intention for marriage. It's to be an echo or reflection of the relationship that exists between Christ and the Church—always a very imperfect reflection, but a reflection nonetheless.

Please don't think of this as merely a helpful illustration or an interesting perspective. It's much more than that. This is the essence of marriage. This is the divine purpose for *your* marriage.

And don't get it backwards either. We don't look to marriage to understand the relationship between Christ and the Church. Instead, we seek a clear, biblical understanding of the relationship between Christ and the Church so we can better understand the purpose of our marriage.

This means that your marriage is meant to be, by the grace of God, the best echo, the most faithful reflection, of that relationship that you can possibly be. It's not about impressing people or drawing attention to ourselves. It's about being genuinely united in a strong, godly, intimate relationship that echoes the one between Christ and the Church.

Has your marriage primarily been centered on you? On your wife? On your children? On your responsibilities? On your goals? On your comforts? On your stuff? If so, you've been trying to live in a way you were never intended to.

The biblical purpose for marriage, you see, is not man-centered or needs-centered. It's God-centered. It's profoundly mysterious and profoundly significant. Your marriage is meant to point to the truth of the crucified and risen Savior who will return for his Bride.

This understanding will help you immensely as you seek to implement what you find in this book. There is a glorious purpose behind the practice.

We're taking this time to review the biblical purpose of marriage because, let's face it, men can all too easily think that a book about sex is nothing more than a book about sex. Yes, this book is primarily about romance and sex, because that's the emphasis in Solomon's Song. But if this book merely recommended a set of techniques, it would be no more helpful than some secular sex manual. What will make the difference for you is an understanding of the purpose of marriage.

As Christians, we do indeed have the incredible privilege of knowing the ultimate purpose for marriage. But unless we grasp this—unless there's a conviction that marriage is ultimately meant to bring glory to God by echoing the relationship between Christ and the Church—any benefit you get from this book will be superficial and temporary.

So we see that there is a purpose in marriage that goes beyond personal fulfillment. Something of the selfless love, care, and sacrifice that Jesus shows toward the Church is supposed to be evident in you as you relate to your wife. Something of the respect, submission, and devotion that the Church shows toward Jesus is supposed to be evident in your wife as she relates to you. That's the purpose for your marriage. That is why God has given her to you, and you to her.

AN EXCELLENT HOPE

All Christian marriages are intended ultimately to point to that greater reality. The final, glorious purpose of Christian marriage is to witness to the relationship between Christ and the Church.

Maybe you don't feel your marriage is a very good reflection. Maybe it never has been, and you doubt it ever could be. If so, let me encourage you to exercise the gift of faith that God has given to every Christian. These are the plans and promises of God we're discussing here, not the vain dreams of man.

God gives us the Scriptures so that we might have hope—a confident expectation of good—even when no other hope can be found. I believe God can impart new hope to you as you read this book. If sin has hindered your marriage, repentance and forgiveness are available to cover sin of any duration and any severity. By the grace of God, any Christian marriage, including yours, can be transformed into a genuine reflection of Christ and the Church.

How does one obtain such grace? It's not complicated, but it does require humility. For although God opposes the proud, he gives grace to the humble (Proverbs 3:34; James 4:6; 1 Peter 5:5).

As the one called by God to lead in your home, if you will

humble yourself under the mighty hand of God, there is hope through the person and finished work of Jesus Christ for the forgiveness of any and all sin—yours and your wife's. God is eager to pour out his grace on those who humbly acknowledge their need for his help. That's why there is hope for the transformation of your marriage, regardless of its history.

So if you approach the rest of this book with a humble, teachable attitude, you can have hope and confidence that God is at work in your marriage. Any couple can "have sex." But the kind of unashamed openness and joyful, expressive intimacy that we see in the Song of Solomon only happens when a husband and wife are united at a far deeper level. And just as the strength of your marriage will be evident in the bedroom, an increase in marital intimacy will in turn strengthen the non-sexual aspects of your relationship. Thus the lessons provided in the Song promise fruitfulness not only for the bedroom but for your entire marriage. Great sex will help your marriage better reflect God and his glory to the world.

This chapter has been foundational. It can make all the difference as we begin a closer examination of romance and sex. Armed with this understanding of God's purpose for marriage, we are now equipped to move forward with our study of what makes for great, biblical sex to the glory of God.

Should be fun. Ready?

CHAPTER THREE

LEARNING, LEADING, AND LOVING

Before You Touch Her Body, Touch Her Heart and Mind

Growing up, I hated school and studying. Well, I hated most studying. But I loved two local sports teams: the University of Maryland Terps—specifically, the basketball team—and my beloved Washington Redskins. Somehow I acquired an impressive body of knowledge about these teams, even as I continued to get lousy grades in school.

While class work was mostly drudgery, learning about the Terps and Skins was effortless joy. I loved to watch them, think about them, read about them, talk about them, and listen to games on the radio. To absorb everything I possibly could about these guys—to study them—was rich food for my schoolboy's soul.

Why was that kind of learning so easy for me when formal education was so hard? What made the difference?

Passion.

No secret there. What we love, we want to learn about. And what we love to study, we come to love even more. That's just the way God has wired us. I loved the Terps and Skins; so learning about them and growing in my zeal for them was a totally natural process.

I still enjoy following those teams, but my strongest passions now lie elsewhere.

My highest and greatest love will always be reserved for God, for when I was his enemy and worthy of his righteous wrath, in his great mercy he sent his only Son to live a perfect life and die a perfect death in my place. But after my love for God, nothing compares to the passion I hold for Carolyn, my wife.

Because I have this passion for her, I have studied her. I've noticed and noted details about her. All kinds of details. Everything from the kinds of snacks she likes, to what certain facial expressions reveal, to this one particular freckle that only I see.

It has been my privilege to be a student of Carolyn since before our engagement. As I have studied her—seeking to learn what pleases, excites, honors, encourages, refreshes, and helps her—my love for her has only increased.

This chapter and the next are about studying your wife and then acting on what you learn. Both chapters, and really this entire book, are meant to communicate a truth that should be emblazoned on the heart of every husband. If you remember nothing else from this chapter, or indeed the entire book, remember this:

In order for romance to deepen, you must touch the heart and mind of your wife before you touch her body.

This, gentlemen, is a truth that can change your marriage.

Nothing kindles erotic romance in a marriage like a husband who knows how to touch the heart and mind of his wife before he touches her body.

Too often we reverse the order. We touch her body prematurely and expect that she will respond immediately and passionately. Normally that's not how it works.

So stay with me, guys. If you simply skim over these next two chapters, the potential of this book will have been largely wasted. But if you study this material, and really get it, that can change everything.

A Must-Ask Question

Some of you reading this book have been married a relatively short time, while others have spent decades with your wife. Whatever your situation, we all have this in common: There is still much we can and should be learning about that unique and precious woman who is our wife, that gift from God to whom we have pledged our lifelong devotion. There are two primary ways we can learn: by studying her and by asking her questions.

If you have children living in the home, then of all the questions you could ask her, this one is especially revealing:

Do you feel more like a mother or a wife?

(If you don't have children at home, replace "mother" with whatever role is likely to be in competition with "wife." It might be something like "homemaker," "employee," or "professional." Then you can apply the principles in this section to your specific circumstances.)

There can be a selfish, sinful tendency among husbands to view their wives as a goal that, once achieved, is then taken for granted. That is how a wife with children comes to feel primarily like a mother. And that is why the very idea of asking a question like this can cause many husbands to swallow hard and consider going off to watch a little TV. But please don't—I want this to be an encouragement to you.

There may be many children in your family, from infants to twenty-somethings. A variety of legitimate activities may consume huge quantities of your wife's time. Health, finances, or other factors may present significant, ongoing challenges. But whatever your situation, if you make it a priority to love and care for your wife as Christ does the Church—if you put into practice what you read in this book—God will touch her heart so that, even when surrounded by diapers, dishes, and diseases, she can answer that question with joy: "I feel more like a wife."

Not for a moment am I denying the importance of a mother's role. Carolyn and I have four children (with four grandchildren and counting). Motherhood is exceptionally important. It calls for immense sacrifices and deserves great honor. But I can say with full conviction that according to Scripture, motherhood is never to be a wife's primary role. In fact, I think the most effective mothers are wives who are being continually, biblically romanced by their husbands.

As for you, your primary role is not to raise your children (or to excel in your career or immerse yourself in hobbies or anything else) but to build a marriage by God's grace that reflects the relationship between Christ and the Church. That's why the most effective fathers are husbands who make it their aim to love their wives biblically.

Godly children, whose lives bring much glory to the Lord and much delight to their parents, come from truly biblical marriages.

As you learn more and more how to love and lead your wife as Christ does the Church, you will become a more godly, wise, loving, compassionate, Christlike father to your children. And your wife will become more full of joy, hope, and peace and will radiate more of the love and grace of God in all she does.

Your children should be able to look at your life and know beyond any doubt that they have the great privilege of being the most important people in the world to you . . . right after their mom.

A few years ago, when trying to arrange a meeting with someone, I had to rule out a certain day, having made plans to spend it with my son. The person I was with said, "That's right; being a godly dad is the most important thing you do." I had to reply, "No, it is the second most important. The most important thing I do is to be a godly husband to my wife."

LEARNING AND GATHERING

One day while away on a ministry trip, I found myself presented with an unusual opportunity . . .

There were just the three of us in the hotel elevator—myself and a slightly older, well-dressed couple. Although they were strangers to me, they were obviously married to one another. I greeted them as I got on, and since they were talking to each other, I began my social duty of watching the floor numbers change.

Although I had come into this snapshot of their lives in mid-conversation, within moments I realized they were talking about a recent getaway they had enjoyed together. The elevator ride was not a very short one, and as they went on talking I couldn't help but think that the place they were discussing sounded perfect for Carolyn and me. I was almost late for an appointment. So as my floor drew closer I decided that under these unusual circumstances I owed it to my wife to violate a cardinal rule of elevator protocol. I burst into their conversation in mid-sentence.

"Excuse me. I'm sorry to interrupt, but . . . what is this place you visited? It sounds beautiful."

They were very gracious, but as they spoke it was obvious I wasn't going to get enough information in the available time. Couldn't they talk a little faster? Provide a little more detail?

As the doors opened and we began to file out of the elevator, I still didn't have as much information as I was hoping for. With my appointment looming, I made another request. "Please, sir," I said, "take this." Handing the man my business card, I implored him to e-mail me some specific information about this seemingly idyllic spot. Then I thanked them and raced off down the hall to my appointment.

As romancer of my wife, I know that my essential role is that of a student and a planner. So I constantly keep my eyes and ears open for ideas to record. I've been known not to hear my name called at a doctor's office because I am furiously scribbling information from a magazine article.

In my PDA I keep track of good getaway spots, ideas for dates, and many other bits of useful information. I know what to record because I have studied my wife—her life, her preferences, and her responsibilities—and have learned what makes her tick, romantically speaking. And I learned a long time ago that no matter how amazed or impressed I am by an idea or thought, I almost certainly will forget it if I don't write it down. These notes are my building blocks for creating and cultivating a more romantic marriage.

To learn how to touch your wife's heart and mind, you must study her. Here are two lists that may be helpful. You can probably add to them.

Do you know how to surprise and delight your wife in specific ways in each of the following areas?

- sex
- clothing sizes, styles, and stores
- jewelry
- health
- exercise
- books and magazines
- movies
- the arts
- sports
- food
- music
- entertainment
- places to visit
- intellectual interests
- hobbies
- vacations/getaways
- and, of course, sex

Do you know how your wife is faring in each of these areas?

- theological knowledge
- practice of the spiritual disciplines
- growth in godliness
- spiritual gifts that can be used to serve others
- involvement in the local church
- relationship with children

- relationship with parents
- relationship with in-laws
- relationship with friends
- personal retreats
- fears
- hopes
- dreams
- disappointments
- temptations

How much of this information do you have readily available to you, preferably in written form? How much do you really know about your wife in each of these areas?

Processing and Planning

Studying our wives and gathering information, of course, is only step 1. We must not confuse being *informed* with being *transformed*. Transformation doesn't just happen automatically or effortlessly. It is the fruit of application and action.

This is precisely where most men fail, including me. And it should be no mystery why, gentlemen. We have a tendency to be lazy and selfish. Genuine growth involves grace-motivated work, even extended effort. Our information-gathering must be followed by detailed planning and follow-through. Romance occurs when what you know about your wife is specifically applied.

Let me tell you about a practice that I have been engaging in for years and have found immensely helpful. For me, this approach happens to work. You might want to consider trying it . . . or create your own. The important thing is that you have some practice that you maintain on a frequent, regular basis.

Otherwise all your efforts to learn about your wife will have little actual effect.

Every week, on Sunday evening or Monday morning, I get away to the local Starbucks. Armed with my PDA and a cup of steaming raspberry mocha, I review several things: my roles (husband, father, pastor, etc.), my to-do list, my schedule for the coming week, the book I'm reading, and a message I've heard recently.

The heart of this time is when I define, for each of my roles, what is most important for me to accomplish during the next seven days. I have learned that if I do not define the important, then during the week that which is merely urgent will rush in, disguised as the truly important, and will crowd out everything else.

For each of my roles I identify no more than three important goals I can accomplish that week, and I insert them into my schedule. I'm careful not to load myself down with more than is realistic. This is how the important is identified and protected. The process is absolutely crucial, but it often takes no more than fifteen or twenty minutes. (Then, as the week progresses, I make sure my plans are still on track.)

Outwardly it appears there's nothing special going on. I'm just another bald guy in a coffee shop communing with a piece of technology, a wrinkled sports page by my side. But I assure you, great fruitfulness flows from these times, regularly and faithfully invested.

This is obviously not a significant investment of time. But without it a great deal of what I heard and read and learned in the preceding week would be forgotten or left unapplied. Without it I would go through life governed by what seems to be the most urgent thing clamoring for my attention. The truly important things would often go unattended. But with it, as each week unfolds and I find myself engaged in activities that are truly intentional, purposeful, and central, I regularly realize that a particular interaction with my wife is benefiting directly from that time in the coffee shop.

So please don't make the mistake of thinking that simply by reading this book you are being changed. I wish it were that easy. But change does not take place until we apply what we are learning in very specific ways, at very specific times, and always in dependence on God's grace to make our efforts effective.

When I was a boy, I effortlessly absorbed information about the Terps and Skins for the simple reason that I paid attention to them. And the more attention I paid to them, the more I loved doing it.

It's just not possible to grow in your love for anything that you take for granted, especially your wife. To increase marital romance, you must study and cherish the object of your affection through the regular investment of time and energy.

As men we are all too eager to touch our wives' bodies before we have taken the time to touch their hearts and minds. In this book I'm trying to restrain you from touching her prematurely, so that when the time does come to touch her body, it will have the deepest possible effect.

In the next chapter we'll see exactly how to get ready for that effective, erotic touch.

CHAPTER FOUR

How to Make It All Happen

Seven Surefire Ways to Kindle Romance

It's 4:00 on a Sunday afternoon, and you've actually done it. Cup in hand, you've staked your claim to a small table at the local coffee shop. You're well-armed too. You've got your calendar, a bunch of fresh information about your wife that you've been diligently collecting, and some brand-new research about fun things to do in your area. So far, so good.

OK, here you go. It's time to make those plans for enhancing your romantic relationship with your wife.

But what exactly should you plan for?

Ultimately any detailed answer to that question must come from you. But in general terms there are things that for most marriages, most of the time, can bring about real change.

This chapter contains the best, most practical suggestions I know of for fostering the growth of romance with your wife.

None of them will bowl you over with their sheer originality and brilliance; as far as I can tell, I've never had an original thought in my life. But because the chief obstacles to cultivating marital romance are universal, I believe these practices will help you. (Those obstacles, by the way, can more or less be summarized accurately—if somewhat bluntly—as pride, selfishness, laziness, and ignorance. I know because I've often been guilty of every one of them.)

As we begin looking at these very practical methods, I want to encourage you—indeed, I want to insist—that you never think of your wife as if she is a project to be completed or a problem to be solved. (Certainly, this is not how Christ thinks of the Church.) She is your lover, your bride, your best friend and cherished companion, and a fellow heir of the grace of life.

This Stuff Works

That said, if we are to succeed at romancing our wives, we must take systematic, concrete action. Let's reject the delusions of effortless relational ecstasy that the entertainment industry tries to sell us. Real, sustained romance, although powerfully enabled by the grace of God, is still hard work.

There are, of course, certain things that are common to making progress in any area, from swinging a golf club, to keeping a budget, to mastering that new digital gizmo.

- a) Review what you already know, and gain new knowledge. (learning)
- b) Identify opportunities to apply what you know. (planning)
- c) Practice applying what you know. (doing)
- d) Repeat steps a) through c).

It's the same with romance. Time and energy, lovingly invested, will increase romance, which will increase marital intimacy. If you adopt and faithfully practice these methods, I believe God will increase the level of romance in your marriage.

1. Date Night

Time away from the routine busyness of life is essential for the cultivation of romance in any marriage. A regular date night provides a couple with a reliable, peaceful oasis in the middle of a busy world.

At this point three of our four children are married. But I've been practicing the priority of a weekly date night since before any of them were born. (That's right, I said weekly.) If you have small children, I recognize that challenges can exist. Certainly there is the matter of child-care, an area in which you should bear the burden of finding a solution if one is not readily available. But also, the maternal instincts of many mothers of small children can kick in hard, leading a mother to think that it's more important for her to be with her children than to take a regular date night to grow closer to her husband.

If that is your situation, let me encourage you to lead with love. These are critical years for you to invest in your marriage relationship. If you have small children, your wife is even more in need of your care and attention during this season. (There are few things in life more difficult than caring for an infant and a toddler at the same time. If you don't believe that, send your wife away on a personal retreat for twenty-four hours, and spend that entire time caring for the children yourself.)

If you do not have a consistent date night now, my first recommendation is . . . start doing it! Do whatever it takes to establish a regular date with your beloved. Go on, take the plunge. Unless it's simply impossible, make your date night a weekly event, starting right now!

A regular date night will help remind and reinforce in both of you the priority of your relationship. Together you will quickly get in the habit of looking forward to and enjoying this time together. Then when something inevitably pops up in the schedule once in a while, at least you will still be "dating" several times each month. But if you start with monthly dates, or even biweekly, the habit will form much more slowly, and interruptions in the schedule will be much more destabilizing.

Now, guys, date night is not about running errands or visiting the local mega-hardware store together. A date night is intentional. It has a goal and a purpose.

So on your dates don't just relax with each other—relate to each other. As we will see in the next chapter, the lovers in Solomon's Song were intentional, clearly eager to know one another better. Many couples seem to be perfecting the art of being with each other but are losing the ability to grow in their relationship. If the most common activities you choose for date night do not cause you to relate to each other, there's room for improvement.

Sure, there's a place for the relaxation-oriented approach to dates once in a while. But don't let that become your standard fare on these critical evenings. Over a period of months you ought to be able to look back and see that your date nights have been drawing you together as a couple, not simply giving you an opportunity to get out of your home and relax at the same time.

Now, about budgets . . . please don't misunderstand. Date nights don't have to be expensive. Exotic restaurants are not mandatory. *Dinner* is not mandatory. A date can simply be a few hours together—walking in a park, looking into one another's eyes in a coffee shop—talking about anything and everything, from the boringly practical to the strikingly romantic.

And one more important point, gentlemen. The date night I enjoy with my wife is my joy, privilege, and responsibility to plan. When Carolyn and I get in the car, I don't want to have to turn to her and say, "So, uh, where'd you like to eat?" If I've been studying her, asking her what kinds of activities she would enjoy, and talking with her about all the subjects listed on pages 32-33, I'll have an excellent idea of what she might like to do on any given date night. I want to show my wife that she is important enough to me that I have planned ahead.

What a joy and what a difference our date nights have made in our marriage! While regular dates aren't the only way to cultivate ongoing romance, they can be a consistently significant way. That's certainly been our experience, and I hope it will be yours as well.

2. Phone Calls

I try to speak with Carolyn from the office at least once a day. These don't have to be long conversations. I'll pick up the phone in a spare moment and call her just to say, "Hi, love. I just wanted to hear your voice. Is there anything I can do for you?" (Be sure to listen to her answer, guys.) And when our conversation is over, I may wrap it up with something like, "I love you with all my heart, and I can't wait to see you in a few hours. Bye."

Calls like this can have a transforming effect on Carolyn. They allow me, in a matter of just a few moments, to touch her heart and mind.

3. Notes, Cards, and Letters

The written word can be even more powerful than a phone call. Do you and your wife both use e-mail regularly? How long would it take to type her a quick love note? You may be surprised to find that you can communicate your thoughts and feelings for her far more effectively in writing than you can orally.

Have you ever noticed that you tend to have different kinds of ideas when you use different tools to help you think? If it's been some time since you've taken pen in hand to express your love for your wife, try it again. Handwritten love letters have priceless romantic value. How many times have you driven to the store, looked through perhaps dozens of greeting cards, and ended up with either no card or one that was less than ideal? Wouldn't that time and energy be better spent in a quiet place crafting your own words? Let's depend less on greeting cards and more on God's grace to help us express ourselves romantically.

One of my hobbies is studying the Civil War, and I am regularly amazed at the depth and power of the letters that soldiers sent to their wives. I can only imagine the impact those letters had. So many of them were written by men far from home, anticipating death. I want Carolyn to have letters from me when I'm right here with her, letters she can cherish while I'm living.

Quick little notes—for all kinds of purposes—can have real power too. In regard to notes, I want to become as thoughtful and forward-thinking as a husband I once read about:

> When the new car was side-swiped on a trip to the supermarket, Mary stopped and tearfully fumbled in the glove compartment for the insurance papers. Attached to them she found an envelope with her name on it in her husband's handwriting.

"Dear Mary," the note said, "when you need these papers, remember it's you I love, not the car."[5]

4. *Gifts*

Romance can be communicated quite effectively through small gifts. They don't have to be expensive, but they shouldn't be exclusively practical either. Giving your wife a dustbuster or a waffle iron might serve her or make her life a little easier, but it does not qualify as romancing her.

Lately, for example, my wife has been enjoying a candy called Spree®. Her favorite is Chewy Spree, which is much harder to get. But I've found a little store that always carries it, and I swing by there occasionally on my way home from work to pick some up. Sure, it's a small thing, but it shows I've been thinking about her and that I want to please her. Too many men try to make up for a lack of daily romance with the occasional extravagant gift, as if to apologize for the past and offer an excuse for the future. I would argue against the large, occasional, and expensive gift in favor of the small, frequent, and thoughtful (although, if possible, both are recommended).

Buying perfume and clothing for Carolyn has been a joy for me over the years, as well as an adventure. Lingerie makes a romantic and certainly a suggestive gift, although men must pick lingerie stores with care; many are heavily decorated with pornographic posters. And while shopping is not something I enjoy—as a rule, I despise malls—I keep a record of Carolyn's clothing sizes, and I know the three stores in our local mall whose clothing she finds most appealing. Over the years I have bought her many items from these stores, and what a difference this has made! When I present these gifts to her, I am always careful to remind her that she need feel no obligation to keep or wear them, and she knows I mean this (yes, I give her the receipt too). I am thankful that romancing my wife has little to do with my fashion sense and everything to do with the effort I make to express my feelings for her.

By the way, don't rule out flowers. At one point I mistakenly thought that for Carolyn flowers had run their course. I don't understand this at all, but flowers still have an impact on her. A dozen roses or a large bouquet are not necessary. A single flower speaks volumes.

5. Music

If you are gifted musically, what a difference that can make. Play for your wife. Sing her a love song. Write her a love song!

But, gentlemen, please exercise sober judgment about where you are gifted and where you aren't. If, like me, you are not gifted musically, please don't even try. In fact, if you decide to delight your wife with your nonexistent musical gifts, you didn't get the idea here!

6. Getaways

I'll make this point again: Time is absolutely necessary to the cultivation of romance and God-glorifying sex. Much time. Unhurried time. Undistracted time. While a date night creates an oasis in the middle of a busy week or month, a getaway creates an oasis in the middle of a year. When was the last time you took your wife away for at least two nights?

When Carolyn and I go away, we usually like to get out and do lots of things. We try new restaurants and search out interesting, off-beat locales to explore. But however much we see and whatever activities we get involved in, I'm always careful to keep our focus primarily on one another. The heart of each of these events is our time alone together: talking, reading, making love, and taking long walks.

For many couples, schedules are so packed that sex often has to be fitted in around the edges of the weekly routine. So sometimes Carolyn and I will go away for just twenty-four hours, primarily so we can have an extended opportunity to enjoy one another relationally and physically. We might do this six or eight times a year. How glorious it is to make love when there's lots of time and privacy! On these getaways we'll go out for meals and maybe a walk, but we're really there just to relax and make love with a focus and devotion that can only happen when there are zero distractions and zero obligations.

Now for me, and probably for you, a brief time of making love can be quite satisfying. But for our wives, the slow-burn eroticism of extended and unhurried sexual enjoyment typically takes her experience to a whole new level. As husbands, we have the glorious, delightful obligation of providing this sort of experience to our wives. So learn to take it slow, gentlemen, and enjoy the process.

So, is there a place your wife has been wanting to visit? What activities do you enjoy together? What's keeping you from making those plans? What's keeping you from saving the money for this very worthy investment?

7. Surprises

Here's a question to ponder during your weekly planning: *At this point in our life together, what would my wife define as a welcome surprise?* I ask myself that question all the time. I'll start writing some ideas and maybe not come up with very much, but somehow it gets the gears turning. Then the next day in the shower I get an idea, then another one three days later while driving. Or I might overhear a conversation in a store, and it triggers a thought.

Every time I get an idea, I write it down. And it all begins with a simple commitment to try to surprise my wife. As a result Carolyn lives with the constant and delightful tension that I am always planning some sort of surprise for her.

Now some of you might be thinking, "Well, I'm not like you, Mahaney." But that's not the issue. The issue is, are you romancing your wife in ways that will surprise and delight her? Surprises make a huge and very romantic statement of your care. You can surprise her with any of the things I've mentioned—a phone call, a letter, a song, a gift, a getaway, or a date—or get creative and make up a whole new category!

But here's a recommendation. Don't "surprise" her on Valentine's Day or her birthday or an anniversary. Sure, plan something for February 14th. But a true surprise is unexpected.

Life and Death Without Regret

These practices are certainly effective at creating romantic moments and enhancing sexual satisfaction in your marriage. But they also go way beyond these worthy goals. How I care for my wife this week, this month, and this year has profound, long-term implications. It not only influences how well my marriage reflects Christ and the Church in the present—its impact extends to the day of my death and, I hope, well beyond.

Whoa, hold on there, you might say. *Did somebody men-*

tion death? Isn't this a book about cool stuff like romance and dates and sex?

Sure it is. But consider with me for a moment the vast benefits that your marriage can enjoy if you just pay attention to some basic truths—universal, inescapable realities such as the brevity of life and the certainty of death. These have had a huge impact, and all for the better, on how I plan and what I plan. These are the truths that make our planning faithful, responsible, and extremely practical. In fact, they make our planning biblical.

Moses was certainly a man familiar with death. During decades of marching through the wilderness, he saw funeral after funeral—countless, endless funerals—as the children of Israel experienced the judgment of God. One day he picked up his pen and wrote what we now call Psalm 90. In it Moses prayed this prayer to the Lord: "Teach us to number our days" (v. 12).

To number your days means to recognize that life is short and that how we live each day has lasting consequences for ourselves and for all those whom we love. "Teach us to number our days" is a plea to be able to live in a way that will minimize regret and the guilt it drags along.

It seems that Moses' prayer is one that few people now pay attention to, for regret is running wild in our society. Greeting cards represent one simple example. What a sad study of culture it is to browse the card racks and come across a dozen variations on "I know I don't say 'I love you' enough." Cards that are intended to acknowledge a day of personal celebration end up being a mass-produced attempt at apology purchased for $3.95.

Funeral services can also become public displays of guilt and regret. After a lifetime of failing to express love and appreciation to the deceased, people come forward to say publicly what should have been said privately when life still flowed.

Unless the Lord returns, someday Carolyn or I will probably stand over the casket of the other. I don't want that to be an experience of regret. If Carolyn dies before me, although I will be grieving beyond what I can now imagine, I certainly don't want to be thinking, *I should have done this* or *If only I had said that.*

In light of this harsh reality, I purpose to ask forgiveness from God and from Carolyn whenever I sin against her in word or deed. And I try to seize some portion of each day as an opportunity for romance, whether it's all twenty-four hours or just a kind and simple moment. I want my wife to benefit here and now from all the honor and joy that she is so worthy to receive from me.

Molding Tomorrow Today

But there are other people who ought to be considered too. Possibly many others. This whole matter of defeating regret has relevance far beyond your own life. Sex, romance, and your marriage are best seen from the long view. Very long.

Our youngest child is eleven. His children could easily be alive a hundred years from now and have great-grandchildren of their own. How I live, how I romance Carolyn, and how I lead my family today could still be having a substantial impact even then—for better or for worse.

The same is true for you and your wife. What we do today can influence many people, many generations, and many tomorrows.

I'm not one to accumulate stuff; I love to give away or throw away things that threaten to clutter up my life. But I have a box in which I put items that I want to outlive me. This box contains various letters, e-mails, and records of significant events in our family history and in the life of our church. These are things that I want my great-grandchildren yet unborn to see and read, things I want them to know about our Savior and about their great-grandparents. These items I store away for a day I will not see and for a future generation I hope to influence with the gospel.

The reality for you and for me is that tomorrow may not come. It's foolish and arrogant to go through life as if we still have years or decades to form the nature of our long-term impact. In a society obsessed with youthfulness, Scripture serves us well by reminding us regularly that death is real, universal, and unpredictable. Despite all our medical advances, the last enemy will always be death. And the most powerfully passionate and practical Christians I know are those who have an eye on the long road, even on eternity itself.

A biblical perspective on death, and on life after death, can transform how you live today.

You see, I don't actually know if I will be alive at this time next week, much less next year. So I don't assume I will be. I certainly have plans to be, and I structure my life as if I will be. But I seize today to make a difference on tomorrow, in case, for me, tomorrow never comes. As James tells us, "You do not know what tomorrow will bring. What is your life? For you are a mist that appears for a little time and then vanishes" (James 4:14). That very uncertainty, rather than paralyzing me with fear, motivates me to try to serve my wife as best I can *today* by the grace of God.

So, in calling my wife each day—in writing her notes or buying her gifts or taking her on dates—I'm not just blindly following some recipe for a happy marriage topped off with good sex. Rather, I've studied what the Bible says, especially in Ephesians 5, about what it means to be a husband and a godly leader in the home. I've examined the implications of these teachings for my own life, and I've let those implications be informed by a biblical view of death and eternity. Finally, in light of all this, I've tried to come up with practical ways to make my marriage actually be what the Bible says it should be. The result is what you have found in this chapter. For me, and quite often for other husbands, these practices bear good fruit.

One final thought on seizing the moment . . .

When our first two children were still quite young, I realized that my commute home in the evening was functioning as little more than a review of my day. As far as I was concerned, by the time I got in that car, my responsibilities were pretty much over until the next morning. I saw my home as a refuge, a place where the emphasis, for me, was on being served rather than on leading and serving with Christlike love.

In God's mercy, he showed me the selfish motivation I was bringing home each evening. I saw that my commute could be best utilized as a time of transition, so that I might be prepared to finish the day by loving and serving my family well.

So I made a practice of pulling the car over a few blocks from home so I could take a couple of minutes to make an effective transition in my soul. There on the side of the road, I meditated on Ephesians 5 as well as on some other passages. I confessed to God my sinful tendency to be selfish and sought to prepare my heart to serve my wife and children when I arrived home. In this way I learned to see my home as the context where I have my greatest privilege and opportunity to serve. This practice had a transforming effect, allowing me to walk through the front door with the mind and heart of a loving servant-leader. By God's grace, I found it an excellent help in building a loving marriage, enjoying my family, and minimizing regret.

God doesn't want you to live or die with regrets. He wants your life, and particularly your marriage, to be an experience of increasing joy and satisfaction in serving him, glorifying him, and caring for those whom he has given you to love, serve, and lead. First among these, and far above all the rest in importance, is your wife.

This is a biblical reality. You are meant to find joy and gladness in her above all others and with her in ways that are forbidden to all others. This means that the highest and greatest interpersonal joy available to you personally has been established by God. And its potential resides in the relationship you have with your wife. For your marriage to reflect the relationship between Christ and the Church, for you truly to fulfill the purpose that God has given you in this life, you must be transformed by this clear, biblical truth.

A FEW POINTS TO KEEP IN MIND

In all this, gentlemen, it's obvious that we have opponents. By far, the greatest and most serious of these is the sin in our own hearts. As I mentioned at the beginning of this chapter, pride, selfishness, and laziness can cripple our efforts to romance our wives.

Selfishness, for example, can thrive on familiarity. But we must not let the daily and weekly routines of life dull our marriages or breed indifference. The marvelous security we enjoy within the covenant commitment of marriage is no excuse for the absence of romantic passion. This book can help you turn that security, so often taken for granted in Christian marriages, into a hothouse environment for the flowering of romance.

And don't think this is some kind of airtight, planned-down-to-the-minute program that elbows out the spontaneous. My wife, my children, and my friends will all tell you that I love being spontaneous. It's part of my nature, whereas I had to learn all the planning stuff. A certain impulsiveness and unpredictability can add lots of fun, passion, and great memories to a marriage. It certainly has for mine. In fact, the more diligently and consistently I plan when alone, the more I can be wonderfully spontaneous when I'm with Carolyn.

ABOVE ALL, LEAD AND LOVE

My marriage will not grow as it should if I do not attend to it consistently. Under God's loving sovereignty, I—not my wife—am the keeper of the garden that is my marriage. This is the very heart of what it means to be the God-appointed leader in my home.

Scripture is clear: The husband is responsible for leading and cultivating romance in the marital relationship. If it is led by the wife, or by no one, that love will take on a different, lesser character. It will not be a love that accurately reflects the relationship between Christ and the Church. It will not be God's highest and best for you as a couple. It will not bring appropriate glory to God. It will not produce that kind of passion and intimacy reserved for Christian couples seeking to live for God's glory in all things.

Don't let this happen in your marriage. Or if it has already happened, it's not too late. By God's grace, you can fix it. This book tells you how. Study your wife. Find what specific practices will most effectively communicate your romantic passion for her. Locations, activities, settings, restaurants, vacation spots, romantic overnight getaways—learn what she loves, and make the sacrifices necessary to serve and romance her.

If the methods I've described in this chapter work for you, fine. I hope they will. But if not, you certainly don't have to emulate them. Create your own! What matters is that you are learning, leading, and loving your wife. Because if you are not intentional in planning for creative romance, it just won't happen.

Think back with me for a moment. There was a time when it was obvious to everyone that you were uniquely passionate about your wife. You couldn't stop thinking about her. You constantly talked about her and to her. You were always eager to spend time with her, going out of your way to delight and surprise her, and you regularly spent serious money on her.

Is your passion for your wife still obvious to everyone?

Is it obvious to her?

If not, why not?

The Bible, and the Song of Solomon in particular, calls us to a godly standard, guys. But it's one we definitely can reach by God's grace. We must touch the hearts and minds of our wives before we touch their bodies. And as our words and actions touch their hearts and minds, much will be transformed. Our wives will be transformed, our marriages will be transformed, and you will discover a marvelous and growing sexual passion, all for the glory of God.

How will you begin this glorious process?

How will you touch your wife's heart and mind?

CHAPTER FIVE

THE LANGUAGE OF ROMANCE

Winning Your Wife with Carefully Composed Words

One afternoon a few weeks after their fiftieth wedding anniversary, an old man was walking through the living room and noticed his wife sitting in her favorite chair. She was staring blankly out the window, her eyes red and puffy.

"What's the matter?" he inquired.

She hesitated for a moment, her lower lip quivering. Then, after glancing up at him, she opened her mouth, and out poured a torrent of pent-up emotion.

"Do you love me?" she pleaded. "I mean . . . really love me?"

Her voice rose in pitch as the words came ever faster. "We've lived together all these years. Our children are grown, out of the house, and doing well. I can count on one hand the number of Sundays we haven't gone to church together. You've provided for us, kept the house in good repair, and as far as I can tell you've never given another woman a second look."

Her fingers kneaded a damp tissue as she paused momentarily, steeling herself for her final inquiry. "But something's missing, and I need to know—do you truly love me or not?"

The old man looked at her, shaking his head slowly in mild disbelief. "Come on now," he said calmly. "How can you have any doubts about that?"

Pulling a footstool next to her chair, he sat down and looked directly into his wife's tear-stained face.

"You remember, don't you?" he said sincerely. "I told you I loved you on the day we were married. And if that ever changes, I'll let you know."

The first time I heard that joke, I'll admit I laughed. But in some ways it was one of those woe-is-me laughs. I realized that the man in this joke is a stand-in for every husband who has neglected to romance his wife with his words. And we all do that to some degree. This clueless husband is really just an exaggerated version of you and me.

Intercourse All the Time

They call it *intercourse*. But the word doesn't just refer to sexual union. In fact, the first couple of dictionary definitions don't refer to sex at all. Those meanings basically involve human communication and interaction of every kind, especially the exchange of thoughts or feelings. It's only when you get to the third definition of the word that any direct reference to sexuality appears.

On this point, the dictionary echoes the authoritative teaching of Scripture. A clear lesson from Solomon's Song is that speech and sex are intimately connected.

Duane Garrett writes of the lovers in the Song:

> They relish their pleasure in each other not only with physical action, but with *carefully composed words* [emphasis added]. Love is, above all, a matter of the mind and heart and should be declared.
>
> The lesson for the reader is that he or she needs to speak often and openly of his or her joy in the beloved, the spouse. This is, for many lovers, a far more embarrassing revelation of the self than anything that is done with the body. But it is precisely here that the biblical ideal of love is present—in the uniting of the bodies and hearts of the husband and wife in a bond that is as strong as death. Many homes would be happier if men and women would simply *speak* of their love for one another a little more often.[6]

I believe genuine romance, such as we find modeled in the Song, is meant to be a growing reality within every Christian marriage, not a dimming memory. And I am convinced that a key to consistent growth in romance is found in the regular use of "carefully composed words."

We communicate with words every day, don't we? Phone calls and voice mails, faxes and e-mails, instant messages, pager text messages, meetings and conversations, letters and memos—words fill our existence. For many of us, our days revolve around giving and receiving short bursts of information, whether in person or through some form of technology. We couldn't function without it, and often the success of our careers largely depends on how good we are at coming up with words that communicate clearly, creatively, and with purpose.

So why do so many of us go home at the end of the workday—home to our wife, the most important person in the world to us—and suddenly stop communicating clearly, creatively, and with purpose? It's no mystery. We can all be selfish and lazy. So let us heed Duane Garrett's words: We could have a happier home if we would simply verbalize our love for our wives even a little more often.

Husbands, it is our privilege, joy, and God-given responsibility to romance our wives . . . really romance our wives. As we look to this Song for guidance, we see that romance involves, at a minimum, communication and creativity.

I'll bet some of you are starting to wonder, "Hey, Mahaney, when is this book gonna get to the bedroom stuff? I thought this was about sex!"

Let me assure you . . . we've already started talking about sex.

You see, what we express toward our wives and how we behave toward our wives in the days and hours before we make love is actually far more important than what we do when the clothes come off. Based on my counseling experience as a pastor, I'd say most wives are well aware of this dynamic. They know that carefully composed words have great power to promote romance and marital intimacy. Many of us husbands, sad to say, don't have a clue.

Let me just test your memory here for a second. What is the sentence that represents the very heart of this book? Repeat after me:

Before you touch her body, touch her heart and mind.

Everything I say to my wife teaches her something about how I value her. Every touch, every kiss on the cheek, every note and gift, every brief phone call—as well as every act of selfish neglect—expresses something about my heart. When Carolyn and I are behind closed doors and locked in a passionate embrace, that moment is either enhanced or diminished by how well I have been leading in the area of loving communication.

So, to talk about romantic communication and creativity is not to delay talking about sex. It is to talk about what makes for the best sex.

Communication and sex are inseparable. It's not as though sex is one thing and communication is something else. Life doesn't divide into neat little compartments like that, especially when it comes to the oneness of marriage. It's all one thing.

It's all . . . intercourse.

CAREFULLY COMPOSED WORDS

The Song of Solomon is a gift from God to help teach us about great sex—God-glorifying sex. Let's look at one of the most remarkable features of this book—how the lovers speak to one another. Solomon's Song contains the finest examples of carefully composed words I know of.

> *(Him) How beautiful you are, my darling! Oh, how beautiful! Your eyes are doves.*
> *(Her) How handsome you are, my lover! Oh, how charming! And our bed is verdant.*
>
> 1:15-16, NIV

> *(Him) You have stolen my heart, my sister, my bride; you have stolen my heart with one glance of your eyes, with one jewel of your necklace. How delightful is your love, my sister, my bride! . . . You are a garden locked up, my sister, my bride; you are a spring enclosed, a sealed fountain. Your*

plants are an orchard of pomegranates with choice fruits. . . .
You are a garden fountain, a well of flowing water streaming
down from Lebanon.

4:9-10, 12-13, 15, NIV

(Her) At our door is every delicacy, both new and old, that I
have stored up for you, my lover.

7:13, NIV

This is miles away from simple chitchat. And it's definitely not
about practicalities like kids, carpools, and church meetings. This
is a category of communication set apart from the stuff of daily
life, reserved for a unique and wonderful purpose. It is highly
intentional, creative, provocative, erotic language. Its purpose is
to arouse romantic passion—to inflame slowly and intentionally,
all the while honoring and delighting one's spouse.

The whole book resonates with this sort of exotic, extravagant verbal foreplay between the lovers. Long before they begin
to enjoy one another's bodies, they excite one another's minds
with tender, creative speech. They model for us what it means to
feel sexual passion and to articulate that passion. The language
is highly poetic, romantically expressed, and exceptionally creative and imaginative. It is also unmistakably sexual.

This kind of talk, which would be divinely forbidden, scandalous, and deeply shameful in any other context, is encouraged
and esteemed within marriage by Holy Scripture. Let's learn
from this book of the Bible, perfectly inspired by the Holy Spirit,
so that the words we say to our wives will create and cultivate
romantic passion.

The best sex begins with romance, and the best romance
begins with the kind of speech we read in the Song of Solomon.
It begins with carefully composed words.

CREATIVE COMPLIMENTS

As we look at the language of these lovers, we quickly encounter a variety of expressions that, well, you just don't hear too much anymore. It's not merely that the language is poetic. It's a kind of poetry rooted in the Hebrew culture that existed a thousand years before Christ. Now, you and I don't normally speak in the idioms of ancient Near-Eastern poetry, and neither do our wives, and this has two implications for us.

First, to learn and properly apply the lessons of Solomon's Song, we need to examine what these odd-sounding phrases really mean. Here's an ideal example.

> *Your neck is like an ivory tower. Your eyes are pools in Heshbon, by the gate of Bath-Rabbim. Your nose is like a tower of Lebanon, which looks toward Damascus.*
>
> 7:4

In the cultural context in which Solomon wrote, architectural allusions such as these were, without question, tender and heartfelt expressions of deep admiration for a woman's physical beauty. And that is how they would have been received.

Second, let's not make the big mistake of simply parroting such phrases. Remember, we're talking ancient poetry. Have you seen the fine print on some of those sports car commercials? "Closed track. Professional driver. Do not attempt." Lines like these should probably be labeled, "Near-Eastern idioms. Professional poet. Do not attempt."

So watch it, guys. If you try telling your wife that her nose is kind of like a big stone tower, it probably won't arouse the specific passions you had in mind. Recall that when Solomon wrote those lines, they were top-drawer compliments! In that day a woman hearing "your nose is like a tower of Lebanon" would have understood it as meaning something like, "Your nose is lovely, a feature perfectly suited to the rest of your face. It adorns your face the way a tower gives breadth and character to the horizon. It transforms and complements you wonderfully."

Let's look at some of the other phrases that the man uses in the Song.

He speaks to his beloved, saying,

> *I liken you, my darling, to a mare harnessed to one of the chariots of Pharaoh.*
>
> 1:9, NIV

Notice how he begins: "my darling." This establishes a tone of tenderness and admiration right from the start. He then uses an analogy that today we can thoroughly misinterpret. In commenting on the use of the word "mare," one writer suggests that the woman must have had very large hips, suitable for childbearing. Another indicates she was no doubt a fast runner! But more accomplished scholarship reveals the beauty and the vibrant sexual overtones of this high compliment.

It seems that in Solomon's day mares were never used to pull the king's chariot. Only stallions were, and they were always hitched in pairs. But in this picture, a mare has been harnessed to the chariot alongside a stallion, and this puts the stallion into a frenzy of galloping sexual desire. So this analogy has nothing to do with comparing her to a horse. Instead, it declares the overwhelming sensual impact she makes upon him. Her very presence drives him wild!

Here is another magnificent passage, packed with carefully composed words and carrying a potently erotic intent.

How beautiful you are, my darling!
Oh, how beautiful!
Your eyes behind your veil are doves.
Your hair is like a flock of goats
    descending from Mount Gilead.
Your teeth are like a flock of sheep just shorn,
    coming up from the washing.
Each has its twin;
    not one of them is alone.
Your lips are like a scarlet ribbon;
    your mouth is lovely.
Your temples behind your veil
    are like the halves of a pomegranate.
Your neck is like the tower of David,
    built with elegance;
on it hang a thousand shields,
    all of them shields of warriors.
Your two breasts are like two fawns,
    like twins of a gazelle
    that browse among the lilies.
Until the day breaks
    and the shadows flee,
I will go to the mountain of myrrh
    and to the hill of incense.
All beautiful you are, my darling;
    there is no flaw in you.
                    4:1-7, NIV

These verses begin with a declaration of the beauty of his beloved. But generalities are not enough for him, nor should they be for us. In this passage alone he praises eight different parts of her body, using clear and complimentary analogies. This evidences some serious creativity!

"Your *eyes* behind your veil are doves" speaks of her gentleness and tenderness. You see, he has studied her eyes. He has thought about what he sees in them. And he has made an effort to express that to her in terms that will bring her joy.

In describing her *hair* as "a flock of goats descending from Mount Gilead," he evokes the image of a distant hill, completely covered with black-wooled goats moving toward its base; so the entire hill seems alive. In Solomon's day, this was thrilling, state-of-the-art special effects!

Her *teeth* are white and fresh, like newly shorn and bathed sheep that glisten in the sun. Better yet, "Each has its twin." In other words, no missing teeth! Three thousand years ago that was a big deal.

He goes on to praise in specific, compelling, poetic terms her *lips*, *mouth*, and *temples*. He compares her lips to a precious, beautiful fabric, and the Hebrew word he uses for her mouth suggests that he finds her very speech a thing of beauty. Her mouth reveals her heart, and part of her beauty lies in how she expresses herself. Take careful note, men, that these compliments are not merely physical. He is also finding opportunities to honor her for her godly character.

Gazing lower, he speaks in tender and radiant language of her *neck* and *breasts*. In comparing her neck to a royal tower bedecked with shields, he commends her for the elegance, dignity, and grandeur with which she carries herself. Then, considering her breasts, he declares with breathtaking delicacy and understatement his unmistakably erotic intentions.

He ends this love poem where he began, assuring her that in his eyes she is "all beautiful . . . there is no flaw in [her]." Perfection itself.

And note this well, gentlemen: Throughout the passages in which one lover describes the body of the other—for, as we shall see, the woman also compliments her man in no uncertain terms—there is both beauty and brilliance. In these phrases the most private emotions about the most intimate parts of the lover's body are expressed appropriately, romantically, erotically, and tastefully. There is no medical language, no crudeness, and no obscenity anywhere in the book. None. Every word is tender and sensual and carefully composed to produce appropriate and passionate arousal.

INTENTIONAL EXAGGERATION

In the man's description of his beloved, notice that we have very few clear statements of fact. We know she had no missing teeth—a real plus—but there's little else we can really quantify. The overall description we have of this woman is filtered almost exclusively through the man's impressions of her. He even goes so far as to call her flawless.

Now, is he lying? Is he flattering her? Does he need glasses? Not at all.

He is not describing so much what she looks like, but how he feels about her. There is a huge difference.

Many Christian husbands and wives have been so deeply influenced by the fashion industry that they find it a challenge to really understand these descriptions. To a certain extent we have been conformed to this world, and that compromises our ability to understand truth clearly. When we read these statements, we make the error of applying them culturally, not biblically. But as romance is biblically cultivated, these really can be very apt and accurate descriptions.

When the man says, "All beautiful you are, my darling; there is no flaw in you" (4:7, NIV), and when he calls her, "my perfect one" (6:9), what's going on is very clear. He is lavishing high praises upon his beloved in an effort to communicate her effect on him. These are expressions of his heartfelt evaluation of her. They are not based on cultural criteria. Others may not share his assessment of her beauty, but he doesn't care. This is how he sees her, and together they rejoice in that assessment.

The same is true of the woman's view of her man.

> My lover is radiant and ruddy,
>   outstanding among ten thousand.
> His head is purest gold;
>   his hair is wavy
>   and black as a raven.
> His eyes are like doves
>   by the water streams,
> washed in milk,
>   mounted like jewels.
> His cheeks are like beds of spice
>   yielding perfume.
> His lips are like lilies
>   dripping with myrrh.
> His arms are rods of gold
>   set with chrysolite.
> His body is like polished ivory
>   decorated with sapphires.
> His legs are pillars of marble
>   set on bases of pure gold.
> His appearance is like Lebanon,
>   choice as its cedars.
> His mouth is sweetness itself;
>   he is altogether lovely.
> This is my lover, this is my friend,
>   O daughters of Jerusalem.
>   5:10-16, NIV

Here is a description that few men could ever hope to deserve. Yet these are statements of integrity because they represent her personal assessment of him, an assessment informed by her exclusive, passionate love for him.

This is simply how she feels about him. An objective description is clearly not the point! These are carefully composed words that convey to him her estimation of his value. What she was getting at is something like this:

Radiant—there is a joy and an inner contentment that shines through his face.

Ruddy—he is manly and masculine.

Outstanding—place him in the midst of ten thousand others and she can quickly pick him out, for in her eyes he has no rivals.

Head, hair, eyes, cheeks—she loves to look upon him. Not primarily because of his objective physical features, but because of what he means to her.

Lips and *mouth*—his speech is lovely (although this also means that she greatly enjoys his kisses).

Arms, body, legs, appearance—he is her man, solid and firm, like a range of mountains.

Finally, she ends her praise with this: "He is altogether lovely. This is my lover, this is my friend, O daughters of Jerusalem." With this triumphant declaration she invites all the daughters of Jerusalem to agree with her. We're invited to agree with her too.

Is she concerned that anyone might hold a different opinion? Not at all, for who would argue? This is how she feels! Some may criticize her objectivity or precision, but even as they do, they will envy the depth of love she enjoys and will find themselves, by contrast, far poorer than this woman and her lover.

What we see in these compliments is simply a purified and well-articulated form of something universally common to lovers. You *should* be special in her eyes, just as she should be special to you—uniquely special, outrageously special, with a value far above that of any other person, a value that others might even see as "inaccurate."

Believe me, guys, how my wife describes me bears little or no resemblance to how my male friends describe me. (Just one example: After teaching on this material a few years ago, a friend and fellow pastor walked up to me after the message, glanced at my bald pate, and said, "Your head reminds me of the Jefferson Memorial.")

This is all as it should be. There is a marked difference between emotional descriptions of one's beloved and the kind of description you'd give a friend to help him pick up someone at the airport. Let's not confuse the two. A man may say to his wife, "My darling, you are five feet seven, of medium build, with a birth mark on your left shoulder blade, and you are mildly allergic to shellfish." In this he may be entirely accurate, but he will not be telling her how much she means to him. And he certainly won't be adding fuel to the fires of romance.

Learning the Language

In the Song of Solomon, God provides numerous illustrations of provocative and erotic speech. This is how we should speak *to* our wives *about* our wives.

Some of us husbands, tragically, are a little like the guy at the beginning of this chapter who thought that uttering "I love you" once every half century or so was probably about enough. Others of us imagine we're doing OK if now and then we say,

"That dress looks nice on you, dear" or "Hey, are those new earrings?" But I trust we're all seeing from Scripture that the standard is far, far higher.

There is obviously a huge difference between carefully composed words of romance and "Hey, that dress looks nice on you." By all means tell her when you think she looks nice, but recognize the world of difference between a simple compliment (however sincere) and phrases describing your appreciation and passion for her.

But I can hear you now. "C. J., if I can't quote Solomon, how do I generate my own carefully composed words? I'm not a poet. I'm not Shakespeare. I don't even like poetry."

Well, neither am I. Where I grew up, if a guy revealed that he was interested in anything vaguely poetic, he would be beaten up. Poetry was, by definition, effeminate and revolting. Real guys played sports. We talked about sports, and we read sports—not poetry, and definitely not Shakespeare.

Just a few years ago, in fact, out of arrogance and deep ignorance I said in passing from the pulpit, "Shakespeare was a bum." One horrified literature teacher in our church very kindly offered to enlighten me. A little while later I spent an evening with a group of friends, including that teacher, watching a video of *Henry V*. As I watched, I came to understand something: It was really me who was the bum. Here was highly poetic speech, which I had once scorned, but it was incredibly powerful stuff, and not effeminate in the least.

Solomon, too, was definitely masculine. Far from scorning carefully composed words, I should accept the lesson of Solomon's Song and learn how to use them. Poetic language is a gift from God that can help me promote godly romance with my wife!

So let's try to bring this home a little. How many times in the past week or month have you spoken to your wife in ways that she found to be romantically and perhaps erotically arousing?

Now, what would hold you back from doing this on a regular basis? What are the issues in your own heart that would prevent you?

Let's try a few on for size. Maybe one of them will fit you.

"I'm not sure it really matters to her."

Wrong. Remember: Thanks be to God, our wives aren't wired like men. The spoken word can be as alluring, provocative, and enticing to your wife as any visual stimulation you experience with her.

"I don't think I can come up with anything creative."

It might not be the easiest thing you've ever done. But if you will humble yourself and ask him for it, God is eager to give you that simple but effective phrase to say to your wife. The first such phrase will begin to break down the barriers of pride and self-absorption that hinder you. The second phrase will be easier. Then you're on your way.

"It just seems silly."

But it doesn't have to. Discover what's genuine and works for you and your wife. Again, don't let the poetry aspect turn you off. What sort of language appeals to both of you and comes naturally?

God wants you, as a Christian husband, to carefully compose words that communicate your appreciation, affections, and passions for your wife, and he will help you do it in a way that is meaningful to her. It doesn't have to rhyme. It doesn't even have to be beautiful. It just has to connect in a way that affects her uniquely.

After I taught this material in our church, one man showed me a line he had written: "Honey, to me, you are like freshly shucked corn in a trough surrounded by hungry hogs."

Now, this didn't quite fit my cultural background, but I was immediately able to encourage him. "If your wife is romanced by this, fantastic! If this speaks her language and encourages her and helps her understand your passion for her, then Solomon would be very pleased with you."

The point is, guys, you don't need to be a Shakespeare or a Solomon. You don't need to imitate some specific style. But you should definitely follow the example given to us in the Song—by carefully composing words of a romantic and erotically suggestive nature that will express your love for your wife. As you do this, you and she will be drawn into a deeper and more satisfying relationship.

What changes, even something small, can you make *this week* to begin cultivating and expressing your passion for your wife?

Now, some of you may be more comfortable, creative, and effective when you communicate in written form. By all means, do so! But however you do it, I think you'll find that after a little practice with carefully composed words, they will begin to come more easily. As you build the habit of delighting your wife with your words, the phrases will become more spontaneous.

Recently Carolyn and I were in a mall while on vacation. We intentionally separated for a while, and as the time drew near for us to meet up again, I began searching the crowds for her. Finally I caught sight of her. She approached, and I embraced her. I said, "Love, I just want you to know that whenever I'm searching for you in a crowd, you are the only one who appears to me in color. The rest of the world is black-and-white to me."

These spontaneous words didn't come from any unique gifting in me. I think they were inspired by my study of the Song of Solomon. Words like these are far more effective than "Hey, uh . . . you look nice." So believe me, God is eager to help you grow in this area. That's why there's hope for every husband. Even those who call Shakespeare a bum.

CHAPTER SIX

THE GIFT OF MARITAL INTIMACY

A Holy Immersion in Erotic Joy

Well here it is, gentlemen. Just what you've been waiting for. You've made it to the sex chapter. I hope each one of you has paid close attention to chapters 1—5. But if not—if you've been skimming up to this point, or if you're not serious about studying your wife and planning how to love her better—please don't kid yourself. If you take that approach, this chapter can't offer you any lasting benefits. The Bible's instruction in marital intimacy is a package deal. The key to effectively and erotically touching her body is first to touch her heart and mind.

But I'm going to assume you're ready . . . So let's get started.

Marriages that are full of rich, exciting, God-glorifying sex are marriages in which husband and wife are clear on some of the basic truths about sex and marriage.

For example, where did sexual desire come from? Easy question. It came from the mind of God as part of his plan for creation.

So what is sex anyway? This is a very important question that can appear to be just a really dumb question.

Sex is a gift from God, a gift to be enjoyed by a man and a woman exclusively within marriage. It's meant to accomplish several key purposes: union . . . intimacy . . . comfort, pleasure, and play . . . creation of life . . . protection from sexual temptation. Sexual intercourse, and those wonderfully intense passions it brings about, are designed to help man and wife form a relational bond of unique, unparalleled richness. When these divine purposes are experienced and fulfilled, they bring much glory to God.

"Sex as God designed it," writes Daniel Akin, "is good, exciting, intoxicating, powerful, living, and unifying. . . . The 'one-flesh' relationship is the most intense, physical intimacy and the deepest, spiritual unity possible between a husband and wife."[7]

Dr. Akin raises an excellent point. Should lovemaking within marriage be considered a fundamentally spiritual activity? I believe the answer is an unqualified yes.

Is there a case to be made from Scripture that lovemaking is in any way less important to a marriage than praying together, studying the Bible together, or even attending church together? I don't think so.

I agree with Tom Gledhill, who in his fine commentary on the Song of Songs relishes God's gift of married sexuality and expresses himself with a surprising and (from my perspective) refreshing candor that's entirely appropriate to this unique topic.

This unabashed reveling in creatureliness must not be cramped by thoughts that it is all somehow beneath our dignity, and that we would be better praying than making love. For this is a false dichotomy that must be banished forever. We do not need to sanctify an entirely natural act by having simultaneous spiritual thoughts about God [while] in our spouse's arms. [Passionate lovemaking is] part of the God-given natural order of things.[8]

(Now there's a scholar who hurries home from the library!)

It is regrettable that when it comes to sex, secular culture sees Christianity as concerned primarily with prohibitions. Obviously, sin regularly corrupts God's good gift of sex by divorcing it from the covenant of marriage and trying to create a counterfeit experience. All misuse of sexuality is condemned in Scripture. The Bible's warnings against immorality and the power of lust must never be denied or ignored; so it's right that we keep them clearly in mind. Even in Solomon's Song we find repeated admonitions against premature sexual activity (2:7; 3:5; 8:4).

But once joined in marriage, things change, guys! In the beginning God looked upon the erotic union of husband and wife and saw that it was good. His opinion has not changed in the slightest. So let's not see sex as merely a *permissible* part of marriage or something to be tolerated. Sex in marriage is *mandatory* and something to be celebrated! (See 1 Corinthians 7:35; Ephesians 5:31.) Sex was created for marriage, and marriage was created in part for the enjoyment of sex.

LOVE BEYOND WORDS

In the previous chapter we saw how the Song of Solomon models for us the kind of passionate speech that can and should take place between lovers joined together by God in marriage. But, of course, there comes a time in every sexual encounter when the couple must move beyond mere verbal foreplay. And beyond such foreplay the lovers in Solomon's Song definitely do move.

As this man and woman enter into lovemaking, they do not hold back, nor does Scripture refrain from recording quite intimate details of their mutually delightful encounter. Indeed, the Song does not limit itself to who touched whom where. Instead we read of the extravagant indulgence of all five senses. Touch, taste, smell, sight, and hearing are put to full use. Solomon's Song teaches us that lovemaking is intended by God to be an elaborate and pleasurable feast of the senses—a holy immersion in erotic joy.

So let's be inspired by this powerful piece of poetry—by the romantic, the sensual, the erotic, and the tasteful but specific descriptions of the physical relationship enjoyed by these two lovers. Solomon has given us the divine perspective on the gift of sex. Let's explore that perspective, so that with our wives we might experience its transforming effect.

Kissing

There are numerous references in Solomon's Song to kissing. At one point the man declares, "How beautiful is your love, my sister, my bride! How much better is your love than wine, and the fragrance of your oils than any spice! Your lips drip nectar, my bride; honey and milk are under your tongue" (4:10-11).

There was clearly some serious kissing going on here. The man delights in the kisses of his beloved—deep, long, passionate kisses. The "honey and milk" mentioned in this verse are symbols of fruitfulness, satisfaction, and pleasure. He's a skillful kisser too; so the enjoyment is mutual. His bride says of him,

"Let him kiss me with the kisses of his mouth" (1:2), and "His mouth is most sweet" (5:16).

These two are obviously very familiar with each other's lips and mouths. They revel in the touch, tastes, and scents associated with their kissing. Their kissing is erotic, sensual, enjoyed, and apparently prolonged.

In many marriages today, however, kissing is often neglected and can all too easily become routine. If your kisses rarely get much more passionate than a handshake, there is huge room for improvement.

So I suggest you take inventory. How often do you and your wife kiss? How long do you kiss? How passionate is your kissing? Ask your wife what she thinks of your kissing. What does she like or dislike about it? How does it compare with what is described here? How does it compare with your past kissing? How can you improve?

Don't assume that kissing is a thrill that belonged mainly to some earlier stage in your marriage. Kissing between a husband and wife is a unique expression of their passion for one another and a unique means of cultivating fresh passion. May we be inspired by the references to kissing found in the Song. In light of this divine encouragement, let's purpose never to neglect but rather to explore this rich gift of kissing.

Touching and Caressing

Sexual touching and caressing of many kinds are found throughout the Song. "Your stature is like a palm tree, and your breasts are like its clusters. I say I will climb the palm tree and lay hold of its fruit. Oh may your breasts be like clusters of the vine" (7:7-8).

Touching and caressing are to be an ongoing part of the marriage relationship. How I touch Carolyn will certainly depend on where we are and what we're doing. But if she's near me, I'll almost certainly be touching her in some way, even if it's simply holding her hand. Touching and caressing are not limited to the bedroom.

A few years ago, after returning from a busy overseas trip that was full of meetings and responsibilities for both of us, Carolyn and I took an overnight together near our home. As we were checking out of the hotel, the man behind the counter commented, "I noticed you two yesterday, and I've watched you today. You remind me of a couple of high-school sweethearts."

Now it wasn't as if Carolyn and I had been doing anything inappropriate. We actually get those "sweetheart" comments with some regularity. People often seem to assume that if Carolyn and I are married at all, we can't have been married very long—as if we're newlyweds beginning our second or third marriages.

When we respond that we've been married since 1975, it opens the door to a more meaningful conversation. What a great opportunity this gives us to testify to the grace of God in our lives!

Gentlemen, I want to encourage your frequent, imaginative touching of your wives (as appropriate, given your level of privacy). Touching your wife in a whole host of creative ways is not just a warm-up to your next sexual encounter. When practiced regularly as a genuine expression of affection, love, and passion, it contributes to a closeness and intimacy that can help fuel your romance and sex life well into the future.

In a world starving for genuine, lasting intimacy, a loving Christian marriage is a powerful witness to the gospel and the goodness of God. Let's overturn the worldly notion that only newlyweds can be expected to make frequent, romantic touching a matter of lifestyle.

So talk to your wife about what she thinks makes for appropriate and pleasurable touching, in public and in private. In this process you may need to lead diligently, graciously, and with love. Do whatever is necessary to get beyond any embarrassment arising from pride that might be associated with such a subject. The two of you need to be able to discuss these kinds of topics openly and honestly. If you're not sure how to do that, back up a few chapters and revisit the material about touching her heart and mind. That will be a key to both of you being able to communicate freely and really learn how to love one another better.

Ultimate Intimacy

In chapters 4 and 5 of the Song, Solomon gives us a glimpse of ultimate physical passion as this couple prepares to come together for sexual intercourse. The restraint that has characterized the book to this point no longer applies. The time has come for sexual union.

Their encounter begins with the woman inviting the man to come and enjoy her love. "Awake, O north wind, and come, O south wind! Blow upon my garden, let its spices flow. Let my beloved come to his garden, and eat its choicest fruits" (4:16).

In the next verse the man eagerly responds. Even here the poetry is discreet and restrained, bursting with passion and yet completely devoid of vulgarity. "I came to my garden, my sister, my bride, I gathered my myrrh with my spice, I ate my honey-comb with my honey, I drank my wine with my milk" (5:1).

Myrrh, spice, honeycomb, honey, wine, milk—he likens her sensual delights to the most extraordinary luxuries available in that culture. Nine times he inserts the word "my" as one by one he claims her choice fruits as his own possessions. She is his—fully, completely, and without reservation.

Then, at the end of verse 1, we find this ringing affirmation of sexual indulgence within marriage, addressed to the man and his wife: "Eat, friends, drink, and be drunk with love!" Here, as elsewhere in the Song, Solomon employs a chorus that stands outside the narrative as witness and commentator. This chorus encourages the couple to enjoy lovemaking to the fullest, to be intoxicated with one another in their love. With God as Author of Scripture, can there be a clearer expression of the divine approval and encouragement of sexuality within marriage?

Let this chorus remind you that when you make love with your wife, the two of you are not alone. God is present. And just as with the lovers in Solomon's Song, God is pleased when you and your wife find erotic satisfaction in one another. Indeed, he encourages you with the same unqualified approval with which they were encouraged: "Be drunk with love!"

There are many places in Scripture where the experience of sexual intimacy is likened to wine or to intoxication. As I hope we can all testify, after an extended time of intimate contact a couple can certainly find themselves in a rich state of marvelous intoxication. (No hangover either!) When was the last time you and your wife drank deeply enough of one another's sensual joys to come to that place of sweet, godly drunkenness?

BECOMING MATURE INFANTS

Did you find the passages quoted in that last section intriguing? Did the images they evoke start to make your head swim? Or were they simply boring?

I know that some guys just aren't big poetry fans. However, if you find that these passages do not attract your sensual interest at least a little bit, I have to recommend that you take a good look at your heart and your conscience. Ask yourself—have you been influenced by any of the pornography, ranging from the subtle to the scandalous, that is so prevalent in radio, TV, film, advertisements, and the Internet? Has your conscience been desensitized?

Paul told the Corinthians, "Brothers, do not be children in your thinking. Be infants in evil, but in your thinking be mature" (1 Corinthians 14:20). So I am taking this opportunity to challenge you to think maturely about this subject. And I do so because when it comes to the evil of pornography, far too many Christian men stopped being infants a long time ago.

Are you on familiar terms with the crude, casual, and callous approach to sexuality that the world calls sophistication? Someday—preferably in this life, but certainly in the next—we will come to see all of that as utterly worthless and despised. As a Christian husband, you are called to be deliciously, deeply, erotically indulgent with your wife and yet perfectly pure in all other moral respects. Culturally, this may seem like a contradiction. Biblically, it is simply an expectation.

Guys, to be able to live in all the sexual joy and moral purity God offers for our marriages, we must be "infants in evil." Many of us need to recapture that lost innocence; in fact, most of us have a whole lot of recapturing to do. To help in this area,

I can do no better than to recommend a book by my friend Joshua Harris. *Not Even a Hint: Guarding Your Heart Against Lust*[9] is the best book on the topic I am aware of. It covers the subject thoroughly and biblically, offering much hope, wisdom, practical guidance, and encouragement.

MUTUAL FULFILLMENT

Because this is a book for men, we need to talk briefly about how selfishness can show up during lovemaking in a way that's unique to us. Unless you just got married last week, you're surely aware that effective lovemaking—the kind that really serves your wife—is not instinctive.

I'm talking, obviously, about that extremely common tendency for husbands to find satisfaction in lovemaking sooner than their wives. Does the Bible have anything to say about that? You bet.

If I am living in obedience to 1 Corinthians 7:3-4, I will take my thoughts captive during lovemaking, and I will discipline my body in order to focus primarily on giving to my wife sexually rather than only receiving from her. ("The husband should give to his wife her conjugal rights, and likewise the wife to her husband. For the wife does not have authority over her own body, but the husband does. Likewise the husband does not have authority over his own body, but the wife does.") Indeed, any married person who rightly sees these verses as commands from God will bring to the marriage bed a servant's mind-set that places primary emphasis on the sexual satisfaction of his or her spouse.

Are you a skillful and unselfish lover? Don't assume that you know what your wife likes. Don't assume you know what arouses her. Your wife is aroused differently than you are. And you must discover what arouses her—and what does not—by engaging her in extended conversation.

Making love is not simply a technique. It's a key part of the marriage relationship. A couple that enjoys great sex, as biblically defined, is a couple that has good, open, honest communication about lots of things, including sex.

You need to lead your wife into conversations where you can ask very intimate, personal questions. Any reluctance we may have in this area, guys, is simply due to our pride, and the solution is simply to humble ourselves. We need to approach our wives with an attitude of genuine interest, an attitude that says, "I want to be an unselfish lover. How can I serve you through this gift from God? What can I do, or what do I do, that arouses you prior to and during the sex act? Is there anything I sometimes do that you'd rather I not do?"

As lovers, many of us have plateaued, but none have arrived. We can all improve. To really find out what brings pleasure to your wife, you have to ask her.

Some 400 years ago, an anonymous Puritan wrote that married couples "may joyfully give due benevolence [that's Puritan-speak for making love!] one to the other; as two musical instruments rightly fitted do make a most pleasant and sweet harmony in a well-tuned consort."[10] This musical metaphor offers a compelling vision for the beauty of a husband and wife who serve one another in their lovemaking. It's an image of a couple who are "on the same page" in their sexual understanding of each other, and who have learned how to "play together" in a glorious, interweaving harmony of passion. This is indeed a worthy goal, involving a journey that is itself full of delight.

Are the Kids Home?

Children are a gift from God. But as every parent knows, they do complicate matters . . . some matters more than others.

Imagine the little ones, all tucked into their bunks, drifting off to sleep, but vaguely wondering why it sounds like Mommy and Daddy are exercising in the next room. As long as the kids are young enough, most parents won't see that as a problem. It's as they grow up that things can get tricky. A couple with a sex life that honors God will, over the years, almost certainly be interrupted by children at some very inconvenient moments.

On various occasions Carolyn and I have been in our bedroom, door locked, in the advanced stages of celebrating the gift of sex, when we heard that gentle knock. On such an occasion my challenge is to project a calm tone of voice, as if I'm reading a book or looking for a particular pair of socks.

Knock, knock, knock . . .

"Mom? Dad?"

"Um . . ." (clearing my throat, stalling for time.) "Ye . . . yes?"

"Is there a spare roll of toilet paper in your bathroom?"

Now, if my children were more perceptive, they would sense my vulnerability at these moments and immediately shift tactics to leverage the opportunity.

Knock, knock, knock . . .

"Mom? Dad?"

"Um . . ." (clearing my throat, stalling for time.) "Ye . . . yes?"

"Daaaad? Hey, can I . . . mmm . . . have a new car?"

"Uh, sure. Let's talk later."

"OK, cool. Thanks!"

When it comes to enjoying sex with your wife, obviously the more children you have, the more care and planning may be necessary to assure your privacy.

FOR A CHANGE OF PACE, TRY A CHANGE OF PLACE

Speaking of bedrooms, let me suggest you try some other locations in your home once in a while. Why not take a creatively mischievous look around your home for some options?

Of course, there's always that classic rendezvous, the hotel. Many times when Carolyn has picked me up at the airport as I'm coming home from a trip, I've said to her, "Love, I cannot wait until this evening, when the children are in bed, to make love to you. See that motel? You and I are paying them a visit." These have not only been romantic and exciting episodes, but they can make for most interesting interactions at the registration desk.

"Business or pleasure?"

"Purest of pleasure, sir."

"Where are you from, Mr. Mahaney?"

"*My wife and I* live about a mile down the road."

Decent motel/hotel rooms don't come cheap. But let's not allow budgetary concerns to keep us from pursuing creative possibilities like these. I can make a good guess at what I've spent on those post-travel flings, and there's no question about it—they have been an excellent investment. That money didn't simply buy Carolyn and me some deliciously impulsive passion. It has made possible a whole host of memories that we will be drawing on for the rest of our lives.

I'm no fan of advice columnists, but when flipping through the paper one day I came across a very moving letter to Ann

Landers. Written by a widower, the man referred with obvious delight to the decades of unabashed physical intimacy he and his wife had enjoyed together.

> I married one in a million. She was totally uninhibited, willing and eager to make love any place at any time. I must say we dreamed up some mighty unusual situations. . . .
>
> This kept up until we were in our sixties, when my beloved wife passed away. I always felt as if we had the healthiest sex life of anyone I knew because we never stopped turning each other on. Our sexual compatibility spilled over into all areas of our lives and we were divinely happy. You can print this letter if you want to, but no name or city, please. Just call me Beautiful Memories.[11]

Here was a couple who knew that creativity—including creativity of location—can help keep a sense of freshness and fun in a couple's sexual relationship. I want to be able to write a letter like that someday.

Now, I'm not encouraging lovemaking in any inappropriate places, or any activity that would violate the conscience of you or your wife. But I do recommend that you two have a talk about that predictable routine of sex we can all fall into so easily. Why not take your next date night to talk over the subject thoroughly? How can the two of you, well, shake things up a little?

That man who wrote to Ann Landers said that he married "one in a million." Well guess what? You married one in a million too. Better than that, actually. You married *the* one. That's one in—I don't know—several billion.

Your wife is the unique gift presented to you by the sovereign, good, and wise God—the One who knew all the details of your wedding day before you were born. Before Adam met Eve, God was planning to bring you two together, for your good and for his glory.

So love her. In every possible way and in a variety of places. She's your one in a million.

REALISTIC EXPECTATIONS

Now, just to set the record straight, I'm not promising that this book will turn your every sexual encounter with your wife into a sweating, shouting frenzy. I *am* confident that a consistently God-glorifying approach to marital intimacy can improve any couple's sex life significantly. But let's keep in mind that we're human, with human limitations. Moreover, eventually all of us will find that age is more of an issue than it used to be.

On the subject of sexual expectations, Douglas Wilson has pointed out that while some meals are steaks, and some are macaroni and cheese, both are enjoyable.[12] That's wise counsel. So let your expectations be realistic, and enjoy.

Enjoy the humorous moments too. Now and then I'll find myself in a situation where all I want to do for the next minute or so is stay very, very focused on what my wife and I are doing *right now*. But then this leg cramp shows up out of nowhere. You can't appeal to a cramp. It has a way of demanding your full and complete attention. So in about five seconds I go from the heights of sexual enjoyment to incapacitating agony. I want to keep my attention on Carolyn, but suddenly all my attention is on my leg. I want to keep my hands on her, but they have to go to my leg too.

That's actually happened to us more than once. What do we do? We laugh like crazy. And hope the kids don't hear.

So you see, ultimately sex is not a matter of performance. We've talked a lot about getting better at sex, but I'm not suggesting for a moment that your marriage should become a multi-decade quest for the ideal set of orgasms. While I do want to please my wife whenever we make love, sex is not primarily a goal-oriented activity. It's an event, an experience. It's about expressing passion to my wife and receiving her expressions of passion for me.

There will inevitably be a variety of experiences in your lovemaking. And to obey God in your marriage is to always seek to be improving. But if we are living with a biblical understanding of and attitude toward sex, then every experience can be enjoyable and glorifying to God.

The Love Behind the Sex

It's remarkable how Solomon's language, while obvious in its intent, is never biologically specific in a way that could be considered vulgar or clinical. As a result, while we can clearly say that the Song features some pretty provocative stuff, and that sexual intercourse is definitely included in the subject matter, we cannot point to a specific phrase and say, "Yes, look, right here, in this verse the language clearly indicates that they are engaged in sexual intercourse."

But that fact is itself full of meaning. Although sexual intercourse is certainly an ultimate expression of a married couple's erotic encounter, it is not the outstanding central feature of this book. What is dominant in the Song is not any particular physical act. The book is not *about* sexual intercourse. Rather, it is about the remarkable nature of the couple's overall relationship—in all its romance, yearning, desire, sensuality, passion, and eroticism.

The two lovers in the Song desperately desire to be together. And when they are together they certainly become very sexually intimate. But they do not desire to be together *simply so they can experience sexual gratification*. They want to be together because they are in love, and the sex they enjoy with one another is an expression of that love, albeit a powerful one. Their mutual attraction is not primarily hormonal. It is primarily relational.

Five times in Solomon's Song, the man calls his beloved "my sister, my bride" or "my sister, my love." She refers to him as "my beloved" and "my friend." I find these phrases quite moving. Their love is comprehensive and complete; they love one another on multiple levels. As a married couple, they have great sex because they love one another so completely, not the other way around.

In a strong Christian marriage that glorifies God, a couple's enjoyment of one another takes place on a long continuum of romantic affection and expression. It's a continuum made up of many points. Toward one end are things like "companionship" and "fellowship." Toward the other end are things like "playful intimacy" and "really serious sex." But exactly where one point on the continuum begins and the other ends isn't always clear. That's because solid Christian marriages are not primarily about one point or another. They're about the entire continuum—the relationship itself.

This book focuses on the romance-and-sex end of the continuum—but without disconnecting it from any other aspect of the marital relationship. That's what Solomon did in the Song. That's what you should be doing too. Because it's all about touching her heart and mind before you touch her body.

CHAPTER SEVEN

STRONG AS DEATH

The Enduring Power of Covenant Love

Yου may have come to this book expecting simply to learn more about sex, and I certainly hope you have learned more. But in addition we've covered a variety of areas pertaining to the God-designed institution of marriage, all in an effort to be true to the teaching of Scripture on this subject.

So, in a book on sex you found yourself reading about studying your wife, having date nights, and creating carefully composed words. When you wanted to be reminded how much fun a husband and wife can have between the sheets, you were reminded that you might be dead next week. At various points perhaps you have been challenged, or found that an unbiblical attitude in your heart was being adjusted. The profundity of sex, you see, has compelled us to examine all the essential biblical realities that surround it.

That's why it is so important, here in the last chapter of this book, to clarify and underscore the energizing force of biblically great sex—that is, the beauty, power, and goodness of covenant love.

Before we address this final theme, however, I want to emphasize that our review of Solomon's Song has only been the briefest of introductions to that life-changing book. I hope that this small volume has given you an appetite to examine the Song in greater depth. So when you are done with this book, you really ought to study that one. But don't do it alone. Let these men be your guides: Tom Gledhill (*The Message of the Song of Songs*, InterVarsity Press, 1994) and Lloyd Carr (*The Song of Solomon*, InterVarsity Press, 1984) have written very helpful, insightful, readable commentaries on Solomon's Song. Use them to fuel your own study of the Song, and allow that unique book of the Bible to have its full impact on your marriage.

And now, back to covenant love . . .

All the sex in Solomon's Song takes place in the context of this couple's loving, committed relationship. Covenant love is the main theme of the Song, without which the book itself cannot be rightly understood. Lloyd Carr notes, "The theme of sexual enjoyment and consummation runs through the book, and the theme of commitment is central to that whole relationship. This is no passing encounter: this is total dedication and permanent obligation."[13]

So Solomon takes time at the end of his bold celebration of sexuality to remind us of the foundation of loving, marital commitment that must underlie all such intimacy.

> *Who is that coming up from the wilderness,*
> *leaning on her beloved? . . .*
> *Set me as a seal upon your heart,*
> *as a seal upon your arm,*
> *for love is strong as death,*
> *jealousy is fierce as the grave.*
> *Its flashes are flashes of fire,*

the very flame of the LORD.
Many waters cannot quench love,
* neither can floods drown it.*
If a man offered for love
* all the wealth of his house,*
* he would be utterly despised.*

8:5-7

"Who is that coming up . . . ?" We know who it is—the two main characters. Tom Gledhill informs that in this concluding section, "We are witnessing something like the curtain call at the end of a play or musical. One by one the leading characters come forward, take a bow, and through a characteristic action or by a few well-chosen words, recall what has gone before."[14]

Not surprisingly, we find in those well-chosen words invaluable teaching. For in this concluding high point of the book, Solomon does not simply refer to covenant love. He does not simply remind us how foundational that is. For the first time in the book he defines love for us. He offers a vivid description of it, assigning to it and identifying within it specific traits, to which we would do well to pay attention.

The covenant love that characterizes marriage under God is marked with a seal. It is "strong as death." It is an unquenchable flame. And it is not something that can be purchased, for there is nothing you could exchange for it that is of equal or greater value. Covenant love is a gift.

MARKED WITH A SEAL: THE SIGN OF COVENANT

Who is that coming up from the wilderness,
leaning on her beloved?

As the two main characters emerge to take their final bow, they are returning from a deeply erotic encounter, the sexual high point of the book. They are, you might say, a couple of newlyweds in afterglow.

When a blazing fire of logs captures our attention, we become distracted by the dramatic flames. The wood itself, which is in fact the essential thing, can be easily forgotten. It is only when the fire dies down that we focus again on the source, now a rich, radiant, golden mass carrying intense heat.

As these two emerge from their encounter in the wilderness, they are like living embers, and closer than ever before. This phrase, "leaning on her beloved," presents us with a moving image of the richness and strength of covenant love.

Over the years Carolyn and I have commented to one another on the obvious difference seen in many couples after their honeymoon. Before the wedding, they may be deeply, marvelously in love. But the physical consummation of marriage changes their relationship in profound ways, establishing a level of intimacy that could hardly even be imagined during their courtship and engagement. After the honeymoon there is a "leaning on [the] beloved" that is often quite striking. It is the closeness, comfortableness, and familiarity that is only created by the joys of erotic intimacy.

So here this woman leans on her beloved, unashamed to acknowledge her union with him publicly. She and her lover are in covenant and are reveling in the new level of intimacy that such love brings. These two have become one, and she is glad for everyone to know it. Indeed, she urges her man to make sure that their unity is all-encompassing.

> *Set me as a seal upon your heart,*
> *as a seal upon your arm.*

Note that the heart is mentioned first, then the arm. One is internal; one is external. This is a commitment of the entire person; nothing is excluded. Their relationship is not about any isolated aspect of life, such as sex, companionship, children, or financial or material support. This is a wholehearted, comprehensive devotion. It's about all of life.

How common it is today for people to say things like, "My kids are the most important thing in the world to me." Well, guys, for you and me, as Christian husbands, that's just an unacceptable attitude because it's so clearly unbiblical. A husband's love for his wife, as Puritan preacher John Wing put it, "must be the most dear, intimate, precious and entire that heart can have toward a creature; none but the love of God . . . is above it, none but the love of ourselves is fellow to it, all the love of others in inferior to it."[15] In short, the love of husband and wife for one another should plainly exceed, in intensity and scope, all other human loves.

One evening when our oldest child, Nicole, was a young lady of about five, we were all gathered around the front door of our home with some guests who were preparing to leave. As they were getting into their coats, I was kneeling down and talking with Nicole for a moment when one of the gentlemen said, "I bet she's the apple of your eye."

"No," I responded, glancing up at him with a smile. Then I turned my head to my wife and said, "Carolyn is the apple of my eye. And she always will be." Now don't doubt for a minute my love for all my wonderful children. But I don't think there is a more effective way for a father to love his children than by loving their mother in an exclusive, pronounced, public way.

Every wife wants to know that she is uniquely impressed

on the heart of her husband. Men, your wife and mine are no different. Do you wear that seal upon your finger as an external affirmation of the seal upon your heart? Do you truly treasure your wedding ring as a bold, unwavering, ever-present assertion—to yourself and to the world—of your total, exclusive, utterly comprehensive devotion to your wife?

It's really simple. No one should be more important to you than your wife or be the object of greater love and affection. So let us do two things. First, let us scrutinize our lives: Is there any other passion that may be eclipsing our passion for our wives? And second, let us give to our wives whatever assurance or reassurance of this unparalleled love they may need.

How will you know if your wife is completely confident that you love her above all other things? Ask her.

Strong as Death: Final and Irreversible

For love is strong as death,
jealousy is fierce as the grave.

Here we see that the power behind enduring commitment is covenant love.

Solomon offers us this potent image because of death's uniqueness—not as an awful enemy or inescapable foe, but as a power—an active, final, irresistible, and irreversible power. Covenant love, Solomon tells us, is a power every bit as final and irreversible as death.

Similarly, the "jealousy" referred to here has nothing to do with envy. Rather, it's a single-minded passion that leaves room for no other attractions. This is a holy jealousy that is passionate about one spouse—and one spouse alone. It is a jealousy that is "fierce," not with anger but with tenacity. A jealousy that, like the grave, simply will not let go.

Covenant love, once entered into, establishes a determined certainty that is beyond all question. A threshold has been crossed. Covenant love is wonderfully powerful and final.

THE FLAME OF THE LORD: UNQUENCHABLE

> *Its flashes are flashes of fire,*
> *the very flame of the LORD.*
> *Many waters cannot quench love,*
> *neither can floods drown it.*

This powerful, irreversible love we share with our wives is fueled by divine power. Although we are the stewards of this flame and must defend it, protect it, nurture it, and develop it, in the end this is not a flame that water can quench. Not rivers, not even oceans. This covenant love is the very flame of the Lord—and thus inextinguishable.

When you are tempted to consider the attractions of another . . . when a marital conflict seems difficult to resolve . . . when challenging circumstances test your patience . . . when you have allowed tedium to creep into your life together . . . when illness, age, or injury limit you or your wife's abilities to express passion physically, as the head of your home you surely need to pray and lead and act. But what will ultimately make the difference? The irreversible, inextinguishable power of covenant love.

In this fallen world, it is certain that many waters will pass over each marriage, seeking to smother its passion. So as husbands it's important for us to know that covenant love cannot be quenched.

When I think of the various floods that could sweep over my

marriage, my thoughts often go to Benjamin and Anne Warfield, a couple whose trials were of a severity and duration that few of us will ever encounter. Having been inspired by Warfield's writings over the years, this account from John Piper only increased my respect for Warfield's godliness.

> Benjamin B. Warfield was a world-renowned theologian who taught at Princeton Seminary for almost 34 years until his death on February 16, 1921. Many people are aware of his famous books, like *The Inspiration and Authority of the Bible*. But what most people don't know is that in 1876, at the age of 25, he married Annie Pierce Kinkead and took a honeymoon to Germany. During a fierce storm Annie was struck by lightning and was permanently paralyzed. After caring for her for thirty-nine years Warfield laid her to rest in 1915. Because of her extraordinary needs, Warfield seldom left his home for more than two hours at a time during all those thirty-nine years of marriage.
>
> Now here was a shattered dream. I recall saying to my wife the week before we married, "If we have a car accident on our honeymoon, and you are disfigured or paralyzed, I will keep my vows, 'for better or worse.'" But for Warfield, it actually happened. She was never healed. . . . [What] spectacular, patience and faithfulness of one man to one woman through thirty-eight years of what was never planned—at least, not planned by man. But when Warfield came to write his thoughts on Romans 8:28 ["we know that God causes all things to work together for good to those who love God" NASB], he said, "The fundamental thought is the universal government of God. All that comes to you is under his controlling hand. The secondary thought is the favor of God to those that love him. If he governs all, then nothing but good can befall those to whom he would do good. . . . Though we are too weak to help ourselves and too blind to ask for what we need, and can only groan in uninformed longings, he is the author in us of these very long-

ings . . . and he will so govern all things that we shall reap only good from all that befalls us."[16]

As appropriately inspired as we may be by the Warfields' story, testimonies like these are not mere relics of history. I know.

You see, I have met Norman and Elma Leblanc.

On the day after Christmas 1965, Norman, Elma, and their children were in the driveway playing basketball and needed to move the car. One child jumped in the car and pretended to start it. But the key was already in the ignition and in the *On* position. So when the child turned the key, the car started and began to move.

With one child in the car, and other children in the vehicle's path, Elma tried to get into the moving car. She was caught by the open door and was dragged across the yard. After emergency surgery that night, the family learned that Elma's spinal cord had been severed. The prognosis: Never again in this life would she be able to walk.

I first met Norman and Elma a few years ago while visiting their church. They had recently celebrated their fiftieth wedding anniversary. As Elma sat in her wheelchair, she and Norman told me that all their children and grandchildren had come home to honor them for that milestone. Later their senior pastor said a most remarkable thing: "I have never once heard Elma complain. I have never once heard her express any bitterness for the fact that she cannot walk and lives each day in pain."

That was itself so affecting. Even more moving to me, however, was Norman's obvious love for his wife. On that day in 1965 a flood of many waters had sought to extinguish their dreams. But as I studied Norman's eyes as he looked at his wife, the flame was still there. I felt like I was on holy ground. I'm sure I was.

As I walked away from this dear couple, humbled by the privilege and opportunity of meeting them, I had only one thought.

> *Many waters cannot quench love,*
> *neither can floods drown it.*

I'm hard pressed to think of a couple who are more obviously in love with each other than Norman and Elma Leblanc. What a joy to observe those who have experienced the unimaginable, who have been tested and tried, yet are living illustrations of covenant love.

The promise of covenant love that we find in Solomon's Song should give us great comfort and confidence as we consider the future. You and I know that trials will come. Let's not be naïve about that. Every marriage will be tested. Many waters will pass over the covenant love that we have for our wives. How encouraging to know that it cannot be quenched but will burn on as a divine flame given by God, who created marriage and its marvelous passions. Because it has its origin in God, covenant love will ultimately triumph over all opposition, all adversity, all suffering, all trials.

True Love Revealed

This subject—covenant love, the essence of love—is the only appropriate place to end a book on romance and sex. How good of God not to leave us to ourselves to try to discern the nature of true love, or for that matter what makes for really good sex. He has taught us about both these subjects in his Word.

On the topic of romance, marriage, and sex, the magazine *Christianity Today* once published an editorial that packs a remarkable amount of wisdom and insight into a small space.

Really Good Sex

While it comes with clear limits, sex is great. After all, God invented it. . . . The first editors of the King James Version tried to give it a "G" rating by their chapter headings, which suggested that the [Song of Solomon] was not about sex at all, but about Christ and the church. But only a healthy appreciation of sex could lead the biblical writer to remark, with evident pride, that when Moses died at the age of 120, both his eyesight and his "natural force" (which some scholars believe refers to sexual potency) were undiminished. . . . Christians, in other words, are not prudes. We like sex. We celebrate sex. We thank God for sex.

But—and here we differ radically with our society—we do not see sex as a right or as an end in itself, but as part of discipleship. When we say no to promiscuity or other substitutes for marriage, we do so in defense of good sex. It is not from prudery that the Bible advocates lifelong, faithful, heterosexual marriage, but out of a conviction that the freedom and loving abandon that are necessary for sexual ecstasy come only from a committed marital relationship. . . . Perhaps we ought to make long marriages our image—our "icon"—of sex. An icon is a picture we look to as a model. We study and meditate upon it because it reveals some aspect of God's glory in the world.

Our society has made sex its icon. That's why it is found on every magazine stand, in every commercial, every movie aimed at teenagers. This icon portrays only well-curved women and well-muscled young men. It celebrates sex for individual satisfaction.

But look at a couple celebrating their fiftieth wedding anniversary. Let's make them *our* icon of sex. Their bodies may sag and creak. Their hair is thin or gone. But we see in them something that makes us want to cheer them on. Through them, and only through them and that kind of committed love, shines something of God's glory.[17]

Yes, how appropriate for us to cheer on couples such as these. But let's not just cheer them on. Let's join them! Let's live as they live and become like them, growing more deeply in love with our wives as each year rolls by.

For this, indeed, is covenant love—the kind of love that produces not merely the best possible sex but a complete marital union. A union so comprehensive, so irreversible, and so unquenchable that in all things and in all circumstances it points to the goodness and glory of God.

The love that sustains couples like the Warfields and Leblancs, although amazing, is no mystery. It has a divine origin. This is not the cheap, imitative love of a romance novel or a sentimental movie. This is *love*. The genuine article. Love as it was meant to be. It is, in fact, true love.

No human love, whatever its duration, depth, or intensity, can ever be more than a reflection of God's love. For human love does not exist independent of God's love. All true love is derived from God, and love finds its ultimate expression in God alone.

So how, exactly, do we know what love is?

This is how we know what love is. Jesus Christ laid down his life for us.

1 JOHN 3:16, NIV

That's very clear, isn't it? Our only infallible standard for love is God himself. And the purest expression of his love is found at the cross, where our Savior demonstrated his love for us in the most ultimate and final manner.

As he hung there, suspended between heaven and earth, he was taking my place and yours, suffering the wrath we rightly deserved for our hostility and rebellion against the perfect holiness and goodness of God. To understand the irreversible nature and unquenchable power of covenant love, ultimately we must look to the cross.

The cross will always be the central truth of your life as a Christian. It should always be the main thing.[18] For your comfort, your hope, your inspiration, and the source of all your effectiveness as a husband, look to the cross.

When the memory of past sins threatens to rob you of the joy of your salvation, look to the cross, where the penalty for those sins was completely and permanently paid.

When your selfishness or pride erupts and you struggle with present sins, look to the cross, where ultimate victory over sin was accomplished and the enslaving power of sin was broken. Allow Christ's love—unchangeable, unquenchable, a gift beyond value—to assure you of forgiveness and motivate you to repent and press on.

And when your hope for the future grows weak, look to the cross, where a certain and glorious future was secured for you.

It is in chapter 8, verses 6-7 of the Song of Solomon that we catch a glimpse of the love revealed at the cross.

> *Love is strong as death, jealousy is fierce as the grave. Its flashes are flashes of fire, the very flame of the LORD. Many waters cannot quench love, neither can floods drown it. If a man offered for love all the wealth of his house, he would be utterly despised.*

This is divine love, covenant love, a gift of immeasurable value, given freely by God to man. Displayed at the cross for all to behold, the perfect love of Christ for his Church is meant to inform and inspire our love for our wives.

So love your wife as Christ loves his Bride, the Church. Treasure and cherish and lead and ally yourself with her as Christ does the Church. Think about her, watch over her, and pray for her continually, just as Christ does the Church.

Look forward to sharing a long life with her as the two of you continually learn more about the joys of sexual love within the covenant of marriage.

Through it all, let the unifying, unquenchable power of covenant love continually strengthen your marriage in every way, that you and your wife might testify to the world and to one another of the goodness of God. And should you someday come to a place of diminished sexual capacity, know that this same covenant love, the flame of the Lord, will be as strong and vigorous as ever.

And now, gentlemen, let's get busy touching our wives . . . for the glory of God.

A Word to Wives
from
Carolyn Mahaney

I can't help but smile when I imagine your response to your husband's purchase of this book. I picture you rolling your eyes and laughing to yourself. *I guess I won't be getting much sleep tonight!* But I could be wrong. Maybe you bought this book yourself and casually left it on top of your husband's reading pile, a not-so-subtle hint that you were in the mood.

One thing I know—the topic of sex evokes a variety of reactions from Christian wives.

For some this little word suffers under a heavy weight of complicated, painful baggage. The feelings of fear and guilt are so closely associated with sex, they find it impossible to separate them. These women have lost all hope that their sexual relationship with their husband will ever improve. To cope, they simply try to pretend the problems don't exist.

But I've also met wives for whom sex is just part of the marriage routine—another item on a long to-do list. They don't mind sex but would be happy to limit the frequency, if only their husbands would concede. Indifference and neglect are slowly eating away at their affections, and often they are completely unaware.

But many women are discovering anew the enjoyment, pleasure, and ecstasy that God has ordained for the sexual relationship—in *their* marriage! The truths of the Bible have set them free from condemnation, bitterness, and selfishness. Instead of drudgery and difficulty, joy and excitement permeate their intimacy with their husband. This isn't necessarily because their husband has changed. It's because they obeyed God's Word regardless of their husband's behavior.

That is why, in the following pages, I want to pry our attention away from our husbands' application or lack thereof. He is reading this book—and that alone indicates a desire to study, learn, and improve. So let's resist that unattractive feminine tendency to nag and instead thank and encourage our husbands for their efforts. Let's get busy examining our own lives under the microscope of Scripture, for God is eager to help us grow and change.

What you are about to read is "The Pleasure of Purity," Chapter 5 from my book *Feminine Appeal: Seven Virtues of a Godly Wife and Mother*. As one of the qualities that Titus 2 exhorts the older women to teach the younger women, I address the topic of purity in the broader context of sexual intimacy within marriage. My hope and prayer is that these words will instruct, encourage, and inspire you to pursue a passionate sexual relationship with your husband, to the glory of God.

Warmly,
Carolyn

THE PLEASURE
OF PURITY

Several years ago at a church leadership conference, I hosted a panel of pastors' wives at a women's session. We fielded questions on a wide variety of topics—from childrearing to counseling women in crisis situations.

Then a woman from the audience posed the question: "What is one thing you have learned that encourages your husband the most?" As the other women on the panel answered, I pondered my response. *I know what C. J.'s answer would be, but dare I say that?* And then it was my turn. "Make love to him," I blurted out. "That's what my husband would say if he were here!"

The room erupted into a wave of nervous, knowing laughter.

It's true! Engaging in this physical expression of marital intimacy and union is one of the most meaningful ways I can encourage my husband.

If you watch TV, go to the movies, or read magazines today, you can get the idea that the only people having sex (or "good sex") are the ones who aren't married. If marital sex is even portrayed in popular media, it seems bland or routine. Our culture has pushed marital sex into the backroom and instead *celebrates* immoral sex.

That's why younger women today require the training of

older, godly women to acquire a biblical perspective on sex. The Greek word for "pure" in our Titus 2 passage means to be holy, innocent, chaste, not contaminated. This word has to do with sexual propriety, avoiding any immorality in thought, word, and action. The word denotes much more than premarital purity. It also includes the concept of sexual purity within marriage.

I've titled this chapter "The Pleasure of Purity" for a specific reason: God intends for us to experience tremendous joy and satisfaction when we express our sexuality within the confines of marriage. Marital union and fidelity allow a husband and wife to wholly delight in each other, without the consequences and contamination that accompany sinful sex. Purity's pleasure is receiving sex as a wonderful gift from our Creator and enjoying it for His glory.

SEX AND THE SCRIPTURES

Did you realize that an entire book of the Bible is devoted to love, romance, and sexuality in marriage? Think about that! God included the Song of Solomon in the canon of Scripture, His inspired Word.

The eight chapters contained in this little book portray a physical relationship between husband and wife that is filled with uninhibited passion and exhilarating delight. This Song expresses God's heart and intent for our sexual experience. If you have not done so recently, take an hour to read the Song of Solomon and gain a fresh dose of passion for your marriage relationship.

But the Song of Solomon is not the only place in Scripture where God addresses the topic of sex. Let's take a brief tour through the Bible and see what else God has to say!

God's Idea

Mankind didn't invent sex. God created and blessed it. It was His idea from the beginning of time. In fact, we only have to read the first two chapters of the Bible before we are introduced to sex:

> *So the* LORD *God caused a deep sleep to fall upon the man, and while he slept took one of his ribs and closed up its place with flesh. And the rib that the* LORD *God had taken from the man he made into a woman and brought her to the man. Then the man said:*

> *"This at last is bone of my bones and flesh of my flesh; she shall be called Woman, because she was taken out of Man."*

> *Therefore a man shall leave his father and his mother and hold fast to his wife, and they shall become one flesh. And the man and his wife were both naked and were not ashamed. (Gen. 2:21-25)*

God made man and woman to be sexual creatures. God did not wince when Adam, in seeing Eve, was drawn to her sexually. God didn't cringe when Adam and Eve enjoyed sexual relations in the Garden of Eden. In His wise and perfect design, He gave sexual desire to both the man and the woman.

Our sexual desire is not evil because God Himself has created it. He is not embarrassed about our sexual nature, and neither should we be embarrassed.

Fashioned for Marriage

God gave sexual desire to both male and female; however, God imposed restrictions upon our sexual appetites. His Word prohibits sexual activity prior to marriage and mandates complete fidelity within marriage (1 Cor. 7:1-9). These boundaries are for our good—so we can enjoy the sheer delight and reap the sweet rewards that flow from obedience to Him.

Intended for Pleasure

The bride in the Song of Solomon eagerly anticipated physical intimacy with her husband: "My beloved put his hand to the latch, and my heart was thrilled within me" (Song 5:4). Hardly the language of a woman indifferent toward sexual relations! This wife exemplifies the pleasure that God intends within the covenant of marriage.

Think about how God created your body. Have you ever stopped to consider why He made the clitoris? It has only one function—to receive and transmit sexual pleasure. God easily could have eliminated this otherwise unnecessary part of our anatomy. But He didn't. He gave us this little organ for no other reason than for sexual enjoyment.

Designed for Intimacy

Prior to the physical union of a man and woman on their wedding night, they do not possess a knowledge characteristic of deep and binding intimacy. They are only acquainted with one another's observable attributes, their most revealed aspects.

The word *know* is often used for marital sex in holy Scripture: "Now Adam *knew* Eve his wife, and she conceived" (Gen. 4:1, emphasis mine). Although a couple may be familiar with one another's likes and dislikes, personal history, character, and beliefs, their knowledge is nonetheless limited. Not until man and woman are joined together in sexual intercourse can they truly "know" the other.

Professor Daniel Akin agrees: "The 'one-flesh' relationship (cf. Gen. 2:24) is the most intense, physical intimacy and the deepest, spiritual unity possible between a husband and wife."[1]

Marital sex is the pinnacle of human bonding. It is the highest form of the communication of love—a language that expresses love without words. It calls forth the deepest, most powerful emotions. It creates intimacy within marriage like nothing else. In fact, as we give and receive the gift of lovemaking, this intimacy will grow stronger and more precious as the years go by. Each encounter will lead us to a deeper "knowing" of the one we love.

Created for Procreation

In Genesis 1:27-28 God commanded the man and woman to be fruitful and multiply. Not only is sex a means of intimacy and pleasure in marriage, but God also designed sexual union for the purpose of producing offspring. In doing so, He is working through us in the act of creation!

UNHELPFUL ADVICE

Many Christians through the centuries have not known how to handle our sexuality. Despite the clarity of Scripture, there has been much confusion about how one can be both spiritual and sexual at the same time.

Because of embarrassment, fear, or negative cultural stereotypes, some have tried to ignore sex or forbid its practice within marriage. Others have acknowledged procreation and marriage as honorable but perceived sex for the purpose of pleasure as evil.

One shocking example comes to us from the nineteenth century. In *INSTRUCTION AND ADVICE FOR THE YOUNG BRIDE on the Conduct and Procedure of the Intimate and Personal Relationships of the Marriage State for the Greater Spiritual Sanctity of This Blessed Sacrament and the Glory of God*, Ruth Smythers, wife of the Reverend L. D. Smythers, wrote the following in 1894:

> To the sensitive young woman who has had the benefits of proper upbringing, the wedding day is ironically, both the happiest and most terrifying day of her life. On the positive side, there is the wedding itself, in which the bride is the central attraction in a beautiful and inspiring ceremony, symbolizing her triumph in securing a male to provide for all her needs for the rest of her life. On the negative side, there is the wedding night, during which the bride must "pay the piper," so to speak, by facing for the first time the terrible experience of sex.
>
> At this point, dear reader, let me concede one shocking truth. Some young women actually anticipate the wedding night ordeal with curiosity and pleasure! Beware such an attitude! A selfish and sensual husband can easily take advantage of such a bride. One cardinal rule of marriage should never be forgotten: GIVE LITTLE, GIVE SELDOM, AND ABOVE ALL, GIVE GRUDGINGLY. Otherwise what could have been a proper marriage could become an orgy of sexual lust.

Unbelievable! But Mrs. Smythers didn't stop there.

> On the other hand, the bride's terror need not be extreme. While sex is at best revolting and at worst rather painful, it has to be endured, and has been by women since the beginning of

time, and is compensated for by the monogamous home and by the children produced through it.

It is useless, in most cases, for the bride to prevail upon the groom to forego the sexual initiation. While the ideal husband would be one who would approach his bride only at her request, and only for the purpose of begetting offspring, such nobility and unselfishness cannot be expected from the average man.

Most men, if not denied, would demand sex almost every day. The wise bride will permit a maximum of two brief sexual experiences weekly during the first months of marriage. As time goes by she should make every effort to reduce this frequency. Feigned illness, sleepiness and headaches are among the wife's best friends in this matter. Arguments, nagging, scolding and bickering also prove very effective if used in the late evening about one hour before the husband would normally commence his seduction.

Clever wives are on the alert for new and better methods of denying and discouraging the amorous overtures of the husband. A good wife should expect to have reduced sexual contacts to once a week by the end of the first year of marriage and to once a month by the end of the fifth year of marriage. By their tenth anniversary many wives have managed to complete their child bearing and have achieved the ultimate goal of terminating all sexual contacts with the husband. By this time, she can depend upon his love for the children and social pressures to hold the husband in the home.'

Some very unhelpful advice from our dear Mrs. Smythers! Don't we all feel sorry for Mr. Smythers? And for all the husbands of the wives this woman counseled?

Mrs. Smythers's instructions were never God's intent for our sexual relationship. Rather, God's grand design is that man and woman unabashedly enjoy sexual union within marriage!

SEX POLLUTED BY SIN

Undoubtedly, some of you reading this chapter have had past sexual encounters that yielded much pain and confusion. If you have reaped the negative consequences of sexual sin—either as a willing participant or as a victim—be assured that no situation in your life is beyond the reach of God's grace.

Just ask Glenda Revell.

Born out of wedlock to a promiscuous mother who hated her all her life, sexually abused repeatedly by her stepfather, Glenda knew the meaning of suffering. In her book *Glenda's Story: Led By Grace*, she describes her traumatic childhood filled with loneliness, guilt, and despair.

As a young woman, she finally resolved to take her own life, but God graciously rescued her. She "happened" upon a tract explaining the gospel, and on the very day she was going to end her life, she instead put her trust in Christ.

Upon her conversion, Glenda experienced a joy and peace such as she had never known. God provided a church where Scripture was preached and where the family of God cared for her. It was there that she eventually met her husband, David. Today they have a godly marriage and four lovely children.

However, the situation with Glenda's parents never improved. Her mother continued to abuse her verbally until the day she died, and Glenda's stepfather never asked forgiveness for violating her purity.

Despite the anguish of her situation, Glenda's testimony is of the redeeming power of Christ. "Sexual defilement of a child is a monstrous sin," she writes,

> and the rape of a child's spirit is on equal footing. The damage from either would appear irreversible. But as Dr. David

Jeremiah has said, "Our God has the power to reverse the irreversible." It is true, for I have tasted of His cure from both, and it fills me with a longing for Him that the happiest of childhoods could not have given.[3]

The "cure" that Glenda refers to is the cross of Christ.

He showed me Calvary once more. . . . I saw the horror of my sin, nailing the Son of God to that miserable cross, torturing Him, mocking Him, spitting on Him. Yet He had forgiven me freely. No one had committed such atrocities against me. How could I do anything less than forgive?

Forgiveness came. And with it came healing, complete peace and freedom—absolute freedom—to serve my God and to enjoy His love and peace now and forevermore.[4]

Maybe you can relate to Glenda's horrendous childhood, or possibly you carry around guilt from your own past sexual sin. Perhaps it is your husband's past or present sin that looms large in your heart and mind. You may wonder if you will ever be free from the guilt, fear, and despair.

But no matter how distorted your view or traumatic your experience, help is available. I would encourage you as a couple to pursue biblical counseling from your pastor and his wife. Because of the transforming power of Jesus Christ, even the most difficult and painful situation can be turned into a story of grace.

THE PROBLEM OF LUST

Not only do we experience the consequences of past sexual sin, but we also encounter the ever-present temptation to lust. Sexual temptation is no respecter of persons. You can be male or female, young or old, rich or poor, single or married, happily married or unhappily married. No one is safe from this vice.

In fact, we should not be surprised or shocked if we ourselves are tempted sexually. The Bible has already warned us that temptation is inevitable. First Corinthians 10:13 says, "No temptation has overtaken you that is not common to man."

Several years back when C. J. and I were visiting England, the media spotlight was on an evangelical leader whose sexual immorality had recently been discovered. In response to this moral failure, a newspaper columnist wrote the following:

> A few years ago, I was in a remote part of the world, alone with the owner of an idyllic island. As the days went by, he became more attentive and more attractive. It was an extremely pleasant sensation. I was enjoying myself greatly. My work required me to be there and my head insisted that I was above temptation. But I'm not. The Bible tells me so.
>
> Consequently I knew I must leave urgently. I did. By the grace of God, I didn't commit adultery. Not then and not yet. But, it's there in my heart biding its time. Jesus said that makes me as bad as the worst offender. Happily, because I have always been taught that I am capable of adultery, I've always been on my guard against it. After all, it doesn't start when you jump into bed with your lover. But months, years earlier, when you tell yourself that your friend understands you better than your spouse.[5]

What keen insight! Let us never assume we are above temptation. We must pay close attention to the warning of 1 Corinthians 10:12: "Therefore let anyone who thinks that he stands take heed lest he fall."

A CLARION CALL FOR PURITY

Because of our propensity to commit sexual sin and spoil God's wonderful gift of sex, we must resolve to walk in absolute purity. This commitment requires no small effort on our part. Elisabeth Elliot alerts us to the nature of this battle:

> If there is an Enemy of Souls (and I have not the slightest doubt that there is), one thing he cannot abide is the desire for purity. Hence a man or woman's passions become his battleground. The Lover of Souls does not prevent this. I was perplexed because it seemed to me He should prevent it, but He doesn't. He wants us to learn to use our weapons.[6]

God does not "prevent" our conflict with sin. Rather He directs us to draw upon His inexhaustible supply of grace so that we can resist sexual temptation and grow in purity. The following are three tactics we must employ in this battle for our soul.

Set Our Hearts and Minds on Things Above

As we learned from Glenda's testimony, it was only through the cross that she obtained freedom from her sin. The same is true for us in our quest for purity. Take note of the significant progression in Colossians 3:1-5:

> *If then you have been raised with Christ, seek the things that are above, where Christ is, seated at the right hand of God. Set your minds on things that are above, not on things that are on earth. For you have died, and your life is hidden with Christ in God. When Christ who is your life appears, then you also will appear with him in glory. Put to death therefore what is earthly in you: sexual immorality, impurity, passion, evil desire, and covetousness, which is idolatry.*

Did you catch which comes first? Before we attempt to put to death sexual immorality, impurity, evil desire, etc., in our lives, we must first seek things that are above. Growth in purity can only be realized as we look upward to Jesus Christ.

Does that mean we minimize or dismiss impurity in our lives? Does this indicate that God is tolerant of evil desire or sexual immorality? Of course not! God neither makes light of nor ignores our sin. He hates sin. That is why Jesus had to die on the cross. Our Savior's death not only secures our forgiveness for sin, but also demands our departure from sin and provides us with the power we need to overcome sin (2 Cor. 5:14-15; Rom. 6:6-7).

Let us never forget to put first things first. Our conquest of sin begins with a deliberate resolve to set our hearts and minds on things above. As we contemplate what Christ has done for us, we will be compelled to pursue purity for His glory.

Make No Provision for the Flesh

It is the close of another long day. In fact, you feel like yesterday never really ended. The baby was up five times during the night. The toddler was cranky all afternoon. You accidentally burned dinner, and the evening culminated with a conflict between you and your husband.

But now your family is finally asleep, and you want to escape from all the unpleasantness of your day. So you flip on the TV "just to see what's on." A show piques your interest, and you pause with your finger on the remote. Although you know this program can be vulgar at times, it's the only amusing thing on, and you think you deserve a little leisure time. You promptly dismiss your conscience and settle down to enjoy yourself.

This scenario I've just described may or may not be a familiar temptation to you. Regardless, Scripture teaches that we all have areas where we are susceptible. In Romans 13:14 we read: "Put on the Lord Jesus Christ, and make no provision for the flesh, to gratify its desires." In response to this verse, each of us needs to ask: When, where, and with whom are we most tempted to accommodate our flesh and gratify its desires?

Now I am not insinuating that rest or leisure activities are sinful. God's Word actually *requires* us to rest, and there are many God-honoring activities that provide us with refreshment!

However, I *am* insisting from God's Word that we never indulge our sinful desires in our recreational pursuits. For example, we should not read anything, view anything, or listen to anything that arouses impure thoughts or compromises our biblical convictions. *That* would be sinful!

Observe David's commitment in Psalm 101:2-3 (NIV): "I will walk in my house with blameless heart. I will set before my eyes no vile thing." The psalmist's resolve was sweeping—*no vile thing*. Notice also that David determined to walk with a blameless heart *at home*. As Charles Spurgeon once said: "What we are at home, that we are indeed."[7]

So can we say like David, "I will walk in my house with blameless heart"? Have we purposed not to see, read, or hear any vile thing? Or are we taking liberties where we shouldn't? Do we watch any unwholesome movies or television programs? Do we read worthless materials—such as romance novels or magazines— that tempt us to sinful fantasies? Do we listen to ungodly music that stirs up impure thoughts? If we answered yes to any one of these three questions, we must expunge these practices from our lifestyle.

Paul told Timothy to flee youthful passions (2 Tim. 2:22). In

1 Corinthians 6:18, we are exhorted to flee sexual immorality. This verb *flee* denotes a very strong reaction to temptation. It is not enough to simply walk away. We are to run away from temptation as fast as we can, to take flight. And we're deceived if we think we're strong enough to handle it. We wouldn't be urged to flee temptation if it were something we could manage.

A woman once told me that she stopped going to her male hairdresser because she found him to be attractive. That became a distraction when she would go for a haircut. Despite the fact that he gave her the best haircut she had ever received, and even though there had never been any inappropriate interaction between them, she determined that she would not fool with temptation. Instead, she found a new hairdresser. That's an example of what it means to flee temptation!

It is crucial that we identify the times, places, people, and sources that can present us with sexual temptation. And we must devise a biblical strategy in order to make no provision for our flesh.

Be Honest and Pursue Accountability

Remember the response of Adam and Eve after they sinned against God in the Garden of Eden? They hid from Him. They evaded personal responsibility for their disobedience.

Guess what? You and I struggle with the same tendency; we are inclined to hide. Like Adam and Eve, we seek to avoid owning up to our sin.

Yet to attempt to hide our sin and escape blame are perilous endeavors. We will not grow in purity if we pursue such practices, and that is one reason why God has established the local church. It is through relationships with other Christians in our church that we can receive counsel, support, and encouragement in our struggle against sin.

If we are facing sexual temptation, it is imperative that we pursue mature and godly friendships in our local church. We should ask people to pray for us, challenge us, and hold us accountable to God's Word.

So let's not hide our sin, but rather honestly confess it and ask others for help. As we humble ourselves in this way, God will use our friends' encouragement and correction to help us grow in purity.

THREE PRINCIPLES FOR "GRADE A" PASSION

Our quest for purity inextricably involves the ardent pursuit of an exciting sexual relationship with our husbands. Marital relations are an essential part of God's plan to protect us from temptation to sinful lust (1 Cor. 7:2-5).

The Bible does not give explicit instructions regarding marital sex. However, it does provide us with *principles* to guide our behavior. So let us consider three biblical principles for cultivating a passionate marriage.

Be Attractive

"In mine eye she is the sweetest lady that ever I looked on," said young Claudio of his beloved Hero, in Shakespeare's comedy *Much Ado About Nothing*.

The husband in the Song of Solomon was also captivated by his wife's beauty. "How beautiful and pleasant you are," he enthused, "O loved one, with all your delights!" (Song 7:6). As wives, we should aim to be beautiful in our husbands' eyes, and theirs alone.

Often women who meticulously attended to their physical appearance before marriage neglect it once the wedding ceremony is over. I once overheard a woman negatively comment about another woman's appearance: "She looks married." Ouch! That shouldn't be! We should give the same careful attention to our physical appearance *after* marriage as we did *before*.

We need to discover what makes us attractive to our husbands. What clothing, hairstyle, or makeup do they find most appealing? And we should strive to care for our appearance— not only when we go out, but also at home where only our husbands see us.

Now I must also acknowledge the reality that physical beauty is passing away. After ten, twenty, or fifty years of marriage, we will not look as lovely as we did on our wedding day!

However, we are given some wonderful news in 1 Peter 3:3-5. It declares that if we cultivate a gentle and quiet spirit, we will actually make ourselves beautiful. Although it doesn't explain how this happens, and it certainly is not referring to physical beauty, it does assert that we will become more attractive as we grow in godly character.

Elisabeth Elliot is a woman who displays this extraordinary beauty. I had the privilege of meeting this author and speaker several years ago. Although she was in her seventies at the time, her regal appearance fascinated me. She had the gray hair and wrinkles that accompany old age, and yet she was remarkably beautiful.

This is because Elisabeth Elliot has cultivated the *unfading* beauty of a gentle and quiet spirit. And this same godly beauty will make us attractive to our husbands, even as our physical beauty fades through the years.

Be Available

Contrary to Mrs. Smythers's advice to "give little, give seldom, and above all, give grudgingly," Scripture makes it plain that my body belongs to my husband, and his body belongs to me.

The husband and wife in the Song of Solomon understood this principle: "I am my beloved's and my beloved is mine" (Song 6:3). And in 1 Corinthians 7:3-5 we read:

> *The husband should give to his wife her conjugal rights, and likewise the wife to her husband. For the wife does not have authority over her own body, but the husband does. Likewise the husband does not have authority over his own body, but the wife does. Do not deprive one another, except perhaps by agreement for a limited time, that you may devote yourselves to prayer; but then come together again, so that Satan may not tempt you because of your lack of self-control.*

As husband and wife, we belong entirely and unreservedly to each other—my body is his possession, and his body is mine. We are to give ourselves without qualification and not withhold the pleasure of sex. The only exception to this rule is for the activity of prayer and then only by mutual agreement and for a limited time.

As wives, we must heed this admonition and offer no excuses. One man has observed, "I've heard many excuses for not having sex—not in the mood, headache, too tired, don't have time. Prayer and fasting has never been one of them."[9]

When we choose to obey God and give our bodies to our husbands—even if we don't feel like it—God will reward us with pleasure. As Elisabeth Elliot encourages us: "The essence of sexual enjoyment for a woman is self-giving. . . . You will find that it is impossible to draw the line between giving pleasure and receiving pleasure. If you put the giving first, the receiving is inevitable."[10]

Be Anticipatory

It has been said that the sexiest organ of the human body lies between our ears. Our brains have a tremendous effect on our sexual experience. How we think influences our sexual desire.

Most of us will confess that before marriage our sexual desire was strong. It was hard not to anticipate the wedding night and that first opportunity to express our passion.

But what about now? When was the last time we spent all day looking forward to physical relations with our husbands? If it has been awhile, if we no longer anticipate lovemaking as we once did, it may be that we have stopped fantasizing about our husbands. When we neglect to think sexual thoughts, we should not be surprised by our lack of sexual desire.

On the other hand, fantasizing about our husbands throughout the day will heighten our sexual longing. In case you are wondering, it is perfectly holy to think these erotic, sensual thoughts. Let's take our cue from the wife in Song of Solomon:

> My beloved is radiant and ruddy, distinguished among ten thousand. His head is the finest gold; his locks are wavy, black as a raven. His eyes are like doves beside streams of water, bathed in milk, sitting beside a full pool. His cheeks are like beds of spices, mounds of sweet-smelling herbs. His lips are lilies, dripping liquid myrrh. His arms are rods of gold, set with jewels. His body is polished ivory, bedecked with sapphires. His legs are alabaster columns, set on bases of gold. His appearance is like Lebanon, choice as the cedars. His mouth is most sweet, and he is altogether desirable. (Song 5:10-16)

This wife's sensual musings culminated in the exclamation: "He is altogether desirable." Do you see how her passion was ignited by fantasizing about her husband? God has furnished us with imaginations, and we should use them to "daydream" about our husbands.

Another common reason for a lack of sexual desire is fatigue. Although weariness is a potential reality in many seasons of our lives, it is probably most pronounced when a woman is caring for small children.

Recently I had a conversation with a young first-time mother. "Before our baby was born," she explained, "I had plenty of time to romance my husband, clean my home, and cook delicious meals. But now there are days I'm still in my bathrobe at three o'clock in the afternoon, because I've spent all morning caring for our newborn! So how do I keep my husband a priority when my child requires so much time and attention?" she asked.

"Honey," I replied, "fix your husband a peanut butter and jelly sandwich for dinner and give him great sex after dinner, and he will feel prized by you!"

My response was an attempt to encourage her to curtail her efforts in other areas so she could devote herself to what pleased her husband the most. For many husbands, "great sex" would top their list! They would happily do without the gourmet meals and immaculate home if it meant we saved our energy for sex. So let me encourage you to ask your husband what is most meaningful to him!

If we struggle with fatigue, let's evaluate our lifestyles. Do we need to scale back on tasks of lesser importance? Do we need to pare down our schedules? Do we need to take a nap during the day? Do we need to take a shower before lovemaking? Do we need to vary the time of day we make love? Granted, this requires some pretty creative planning, but it's vital that we make these changes if we are to anticipate lovemaking.

By now I hope you realize where all this "anticipation" is headed. Our longing should culminate in what Proverbs 5:19 describes as intoxicating sex! Husbands desire more than merely having their biological needs met by a bored, passive wife. Rather, they delight in our initiation of the lovemaking experience, and they derive great pleasure when we are eager and excited during the act. But don't just take my word for it! Ask your husband today what would most enhance the sexual experience for him.

Let me add here that I have occasionally counseled women whose husbands had less desire for sexual relations than they had. This challenging situation can often produce confusion, pain, and even fear. However, it need not hinder you from pursuing a God-glorifying marriage. Again, I would encourage you and your husband to seek godly counsel from your pastor and his wife. And remember to put your trust in God: He is at work in your marriage for your good and His glory (Rom. 8:28).

THE PLEASURE OF PURITY

"One of the greatest gifts a person can give his or her mate in marriage is exclusive and exciting sex,"[11] writes Dr. Daniel Akin. As we have discovered in this chapter, "exclusive sex"— purity within the marriage covenant—is intended by God, not to inhibit our pleasure, but to enhance our pleasure. Making ourselves attractive, being available, and anticipating lovemaking will all foster "exciting sex" with our spouse!

However, having taught this material on numerous occasions, I am aware that not all wives will be thrilled with this message. Perhaps you are one of them. "Pleasure" might not be uppermost in your mind as you contemplate this topic. Maybe this was the chapter your husband most wanted you to read—and the one you most wanted to avoid.

Are you weighed down by a lack of faith? *My sexual desire will never approximate that of my husband's!* Do you feel immobilized by the amount of deficiency that has been exposed? *I will never be able to make all those changes!* Or does past or present sexual sin still appear as an insurmountable obstacle in your view? *My situation is beyond all hope!*

May I implore you not to despair? These thoughts and feelings are contrary to the truth of God's Word. Please be persuaded that God is able to renew your sexual desire, empower you to change, and revive you with hope. You can trust the Savior to gradually transform your sexual relationship with your husband. Remember that sex was God's idea in the first place, and He is passionately committed to blessing the marriage bed, for our pleasure and His glory.

In conclusion, I cannot think of more fitting, moving words to leave you with than those of Robert Farrar Capon:

> The bed is the heart of the home, the arena of love, the seedbed of life, and the one constant point of meeting. It is the place where, night-by-night, forgiveness and fair speech return that the sun may not go down on our wrath; where the perfunctory kiss and the entirely ceremonial pat on the backside become unction and grace. It is the oldest, friendliest thing in anybody's marriage, the first used and the last left, and no one can praise it enough.[12]

Resource Materials

Recommended Tapes and Books

A Song of Joy: Romance and Sexual Intimacy in Marriage
Sovereign Grace Ministries — Audio Series

Here is the marriage seminar that inspired the book *Sex, Romance, and the Glory of God: What Every Christian Husband Needs to Know*. Romance and sexual intimacy are gifts that God has given to married couples—gifts to be treasured, pursued, and enjoyed for as long as they both shall live. Here in five compelling messages from C. J. and Carolyn Mahaney is wise, godly, encouraging counsel, drawn from the Songs of Songs and applicable to every Christian marriage. Available from the Sovereign Grace store. *www.sovereigngracestore.com*

According to Plan
Sovereign Grace Ministries — Audio Series

An earlier marriage seminar from C. J. and Carolyn Mahaney that includes the material on God's purpose for marriage, from Chapter 2 of the book *Sex, Romance, and the Glory of God: What Every Christian Husband Needs to Know.* Is your marriage following the biblical blueprint? Let this encouraging and grace-filled mini-seminar help your marriage bloom. Messages include "God's Purpose and Pattern for Marriage" (C. J.), "Biblical Submission" (Carolyn), and "A Husband's Responsibilities" (C. J.). Available from the Sovereign Grace store. *www.sovereigngracestore.com*

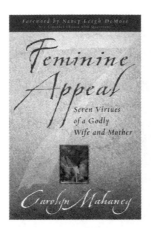

Feminine Appeal
Crossway Books

In this book Carolyn Mahaney identifies with the challenges facing women in today's world and meets them with the guidance of God's Word. God has given older women the responsibility to help younger women develop the feminine virtues described in Titus 2. These seven virtues have transformed Mahaney's life and the lives of countless other women. (*Sex, Romance, and the Glory of God: What Every Christian Husband Needs to Know* includes Chapter 5 from *Feminine Appeal*. Also, both of the above audio series contain material found in this book.)

Christ & Him Crucified—The Passion of the Christ *Edition*
Sovereign Grace Ministries — Audio Series

The movie *The Passion of the Christ* stunned the film industry and the nation with its unprecedented, runaway success. While the film highlights the physical suffering of the Savior at his crucifixion, it does not state clearly why it happened, why it mattered, or what was accomplished once and for all by the death of Jesus. When the film was first released, C. J. Mahaney preached a three-part series referencing the film and clarifying those points. Messages include "The Cup" (about Gethsemane), "The Cry" ("My God, my God, why have you forsaken me?"), and "The Mediator." Available on CD or as downloadable MP3 files from *www.sovereigngracestore.com*.

Humility (True Greatness)
Sovereign Grace Ministries — Audio Series

What does it mean to be great? What does it mean to be humble?

From the ancient Israelites to the brothers James and John, who wished to be the greatest among Jesus' disciples, this two-message series from C. J. Mahaney unpacks essential biblical teachings on pride and humility and offers a highly practical road map to personal change.

True greatness? True humility? They're the same thing.

Available on CD or cassette, or as downloadable MP3 files from *www.sovereigngracestore.com*.

RECOMMENDED MUSIC

Upward: The Bob Kauflin Hymns Project
Sovereign Grace Music

This recording is from the principal worship leader at Covenant Life Church in Gaithersburg, Maryland. Bob Kauflin (a founding member of GLAD) selected, adapted, and arranged these songs—some of them familiar, some new, and some newly revised. Featuring diverse musical styles, plus a devotional from Bob for each song, this collection contains life-changing truth for all ages. Available on CD or as downloadable MP3 files from *www.sovereigngracestore.com*. Free sheet music also available.

All We Long to See
Sovereign Grace Music

All We Long to See is the ninth release in the Come & Worship series from Sovereign Grace Music and builds on the modern worship sound that has attracted national radio exposure for previous projects in the series. The focus of each new song on *All We Long to See* is a life lived for Another—for the One who died, rose, and will come again. From the opening declaration of "Jesus, My Only Hope" to the closing celebration of "The Audience of One," these songs bring a message that help us experience and express the glorious mystery of the Savior. Available from *www.sovereigngracestore.com*. Free sheet music also available.

NOTES

NOTES FOR *SEX, ROMANCE, AND THE GLORY OF GOD*

1. Lloyd Carr, *The Song of Solomon* (Downers Grove, IL: InterVarsity Press, 1984), p. 49.

2. Tom Gledhill, *The Message of the Song of Songs* (Downers Grove, IL: InterVarsity Press, 1994), p. 23.

3. On the vital topic of the local church, I strongly recommend you read Mark Dever's *Nine Marks of a Healthy Church* (Wheaton, IL: Crossway Books, 2000; revised/expanded edition upcoming) as well as Donald Whitney's *Spiritual Disciplines Within the Church* (Chicago: Moody, 1996).

4. From *Westminster Shorter Catechism*, Question 1.

5. Quoted from Jack Canfield and Mark Victor Hansen, *A 2nd Helping of Chicken Soup for the Soul* (Deerfield Beach, FL: Health Communications, 1994).

6. Duane Garrett, *Proverbs, Ecclesiastes, Song of Solomon*, The New American Commentary (Nashville: Broadman, 1993) p. 379.

7. Daniel L. Akin, "Sermon: The Beauty and Blessings of the Christian Bedroom," *The Southern Baptist Journal of Theology*, Vol. 6, No. 1, Spring 2002, p. 94.

8. Gledhill, *The Message of the Song of Songs*, p. 171.

9. Joshua Harris, *Not Even a Hint: Guarding Your Heart Against Lust* (Sisters, OR: Multnomah, 2003).

10. Leland Ryken, *Worldly Saints* (Grand Rapids, MI: Zondervan, 1986), p. 44.

11. *Washington Post*, March 4, 1986, p. B9.

12. Douglas Wilson, *Reforming Marriage* (Moscow, ID: Canon Press, 1995) p. 83.

13. Carr, *The Song of Solomon*, p. 53.

14. Robert Davidson, quoted in Gledhill, *The Message of the Song of Songs*, p. 219.

15. Ryken, *Worldly Saints,* p. 51.

16. John Piper, *Future Grace* (Sisters, OR: Multnomah, 1995) p. 176.

17. William Frey, "Really Good Sex," *Christianity Today* (August 19, 1991), guest editorial.

18. In *The Cross Centered Life* (Sisters, OR: Multnomah, 2002), I have tried to make a clear, simple case for maintaining the centrality of the cross of Christ in all of life.

NOTES FOR A WORD TO WIVES
FROM CAROLYN MAHANEY

1. Daniel L. Akin, "Sermon: The Beauty and Blessings of the Christian Bedroom, Song of Solomon 4:1—5:1," *The Southern Baptist Journal of Theology*, Vol. 6, No. 1, Spring 2002, p. 94.

2. Ruth Smythers, "Instruction and Advice for the Young Bride," *The Madison Institute Newsletter*, Fall 1894, copyright 1894 by The Madison Institute (New York: Spiritual Guidance Press).

3. Glenda Revell, *Glenda's Story: Led by Grace* (Lincoln, Neb.: Gateway to Joy, 1997), p. 41.

4. Ibid., p. 98.

5. Anne Atkins, *The Daily Telegraph*, quoted by John Hosier in a sermon, "Being Servants of God," at Newfrontiers Leaders' and Wives' Conference, 1999.

6. Elisabeth Elliot, *Passion and Purity* (Grand Rapids, Mich.: Fleming H. Revell, division of Baker Book House, 2000), p. 26.

7. Charles Spurgeon, *Psalms*, Vol. 2, The Crossway Classic Commentaries, Alister McGrath and J. I. Packer, eds. (Wheaton, Ill.: Crossway Books, 1993), p. 61.

8. William Shakespeare, *Much Ado About Nothing*, Shakespeare.com, copyright 2000 by Dana Spradley, publisher. Originally taken from *Complete Moby Shakespeare*.

9. Source unknown.

10. Elisabeth Elliot, *Let Me Be a Woman* (Wheaton, Ill.: Tyndale House, 1987), pp. 169-170.

11. Akin, "Beauty and Blessings," *Southern Baptist Journal of Theology*, p. 98.

12. Robert Farrar Capon, quoted in Debra Evans, *The Mystery of Womanhood* (Wheaton, Ill.: Crossway Books, 1987), p. 265.